By The Way

A snapshot diagnosis of the inner-city dilemma

(The modern day "By-Ways")

Dr. Preston Williams II

Copyright © 2002 by Dr. Preston Williams II

By The Way
by Dr. Preston Williams II

Printed in the United States of America

Library of Congress Control Number: 2002104942
ISBN 1-591600-83-9

All rights reserved. No part of this publication may be reproduced or transmitted in any form or by any means without written permission of the publisher.

Unless otherwise indicated, Bible quotations are taken from Hebrew-Greek Key Study Bible, King James Version. Copyright © 1984, 1991 by AMG Publishers.

Xulon Press
11350 Random Hills Road
Suite 800
Fairfax, VA 22030
(703) 279-6511
XulonPress.com

To order additional copies, call 1-866-909-BOOK (2665).

Thank you for your support.

Seek The Peace —

Ahmad II

Dedication

In loving memory of a woman who meant the world to me, my mother, Pearl Brown-Williams *(March 10, 1926 - May 25, 2000)*. Thank you for being a nurturer and supporter of my dreams, and for never giving up on me even in the midnight hours of my life. Even now, I can still hear your edifying words ringing in my memories of you.

Acknowledgements

To my lovely wife Jacqueline, you've been blessed with the virtue of understanding and patience. Thank you for allowing me the freedom to explore and fulfill the destiny allotted to my life according to the plan and pace of God. A special thanks to Dr. Charles Travis, President of Logos-Beacon University, Jacksonville, Florida, for recognizing the worth of this manuscript and including it as an academic text to be used as a part the Logos-Beacon University's "Urban Evangelism" curriculum. To Dr. Robert Thomson, Academic Assistant, Logos-Beacon University, thank you for encouraging me to record the discoveries through my personal experiences of planting an inner city ministry and for being a wonderful mentor throughout my doctoral work. To the members of Generational Empowerment Ministries who have shared their extraordinary lives with me and has allowed me to minister to them as pastor and show them Jesus.

Foreword

"Let your light so shine before men, that they may see your good works, and glorify your Father which is in Heaven."

In my humble opinion, there isn't anything more satisfying and rewarding to a hungry believer, or an anxious convert, than to be able to bask in, and receive knowledge through the divine light of God's revelations. It is the will of God that we become illuminated with the knowledge of His Word, and I am so grateful (and yet hungry for) the precious revelations that He is pouring out in these last days.

More and more, we can see the need for God's witnesses and workers to come to the forefronts of society and share the message of Jesus Christ to the lost, the hurting, and the challenged. I am convinced today that Dr. Preston Williams II is a light for this present age, and I thank the Lord for this spirit-filled, twenty-first century leader and teacher.

The mandate in Matthew 28:19 that has been issued to the church is one of tremendous importance. Jesus instructs us to "Go ye therefore, and teach all nations," to go forth and carry the message of hope and change into all the world; to carry the important message of *observation* into the highways and hedges. Not only does this include the urban communities, it focuses on it. In this powerful book that Dr. Williams has obviously been commissioned by God to write, the core of the urban community's need is addressed with intense and paternal compassion and love. It is clear that the hand of the Lord is upon this great work, and we must applaud the humility of the author for yielding and submitting himself to the will of God, to be used in such a powerful way. When we read, '*By The Way,*' we are carried onto the very streets that are traveled by people whose daily challenge is just to survive. This book speaks with the candor and reality of a bleeding wound, while at the same time, it renders tender compassion along with eye opening truths that grip the heart and elevates the mind. Every heart that reads this material will be uniquely blessed and edified.

As your spirit-man is fed through the pages of this literary restaurant, please remember that the same mandate issued to Dr. Williams, is relevant to you and I. We must all accept the challenge of bringing about restoration, healing and deliverance to everyone we meet-By *The Way*.

Pastor Matthew M. Odum, Sr.
Temple of Glory Community Church
Savannah, Georgia

In his book *By The Way* Dr. Preston Williams takes us beyond the theoretical and hypothetical to the hands-on and feet-on-the-street knowledge of his subject. His presuppositions and conclusions are based on real-life data and experience. Few have written as pointedly on the subject of "the city" and its need for true renewal through a confrontation with the Gospel and the power of the Holy Spirit to change lives, homes, communities and then cities. This book is a must read for every student interested in working in an

Foreword

urban center and those already engaged in urban ministry.

Thank you, Dr. Williams, for your insight, vision and passion for this very needy and neglected discipline.

Dr. Charles Travis
President
Logos Christian College & Graduate Schools

Contents

Dedication v
Acknowledgements vii
Foreword ix

Introduction: *The Problem, The Mandate, and The Paradigm Shift* 15

   I. Cheap Talk ... No Labor 21
      A. The Modern Church: A Fortress of Exclusion (Prejudice) or A Fortress of Inclusion (Hope) 21
      B. Connect The Dots (Melding A Fragmented Social Structure) 25

   II. Restoring Dashed Dreams 31
      A. "I'm Ok, You're Ok?" 31
      B. Dust Off Your Dreams 36

   III. Healing Inner Conflict 41
      A. Counseling: The Integration of Psychology and Spirituality 41
      B. The Word: Modern Day Manna in Counseling 47

   IV. Preserving The Seed 51
      A. Breaking Generational Strongholds 51
      B. Establishing Generational Covenants 56

V. Empowering The Seed 61
   A. The Impact of Proper Leadership and Positive
      Role Models 61
   B. Speaking Life into Their Future 66

VI. Seek The Peace 69
   A. Why Should I Care? 69

VII. Prayer: Entering The Secret Place For The Work Of Ministry 79
   A. Introspection Prayer: Self-inspection,
      The Clean Heart Principle 80
   B. Intercessory Prayer: Waging War In The
      Heavenlies For Your City 83

Conclusion 89
Appendix 95
Bibliography 103

INTRODUCTION

The Problem, The Mandate, and The Paradigm Shift

Inner-city... urban dwellers... the war zone, there are many terms used to describe these individuals and their demographics. But what ever you chose to call them they are the forgotten souls of our era. As I ride through the neighborhoods of West Palm Beach, eat at the restaurants, and minister to these forgotten souls the following issues challenge me to rethink my goals, and engage in the true mandate of ministry and turn my eyes to the "by-ways" harvest.

Why have local congregations not adequately responded to the challenge of inner city ministry? Does it require visionary churches that choose not to play it safe but to take risks and trust God? No matter how you describe your church's social status (your so called target group), I'm convinced that we are all mandated to extend healing toward the inner city to some degree or another. Additionally, I believe God's will for many of us points to direct interaction and influence in the inner city. The inner cities are our modern day "byways." In the gospel of Luke, the writer clearly states the divine mandate, "And the lord said unto the servant, Go out into the highways and hedges (byways), and compel them to come in, that my house may be filled" (14:23).

Neglect is a gross sin that many professing Christians, including pastors and lay leaders, commit on a daily basis. The inner city echoes the pain of this travesty. Hear the cry of the "byways" through the voice of the Apostle Paul, *"For the earnest expectation of the creature waiteth for the manifestation of the sons of God"* (Rom 8:19). Jesus said, "Verily I say unto you, inasmuch as ye have done it unto one of the least of these my brethren, ye have done it unto me" (Matthew 25:40). If God's people are going to make a difference in our world, as Scripture clearly requires, then a new engagement in ministry will be necessary. A revival of our missionary zeal must be ignited. Taking a look at many of our denominations, upward mobility, success and institutionalization changed the urban focus and social witness of the Church. Church growth and urban fear caused many churches to abandon the inner city and follow their members to the suburbs.[1] The masses that were left behind are caught in the many distresses of the inner city. Today we see them reaching out to the modern churches for ministry and are being turned away or redirected to other ministry sources that may or may not provide adequate spiritual nurturing. Why? Simply because they do not fit the socio-economic profile of their ministry structure.

We are instructed by Jeremiah to seek the peace and welfare of the city where God has sent us, "for in its welfare you will find your welfare" (29:7, RSV). If the peace and welfare of the city is one of God's concerns, and if God has sent us to the city to make a difference, we need a clear vision of God's Kingdom in the streets. Isaiah had a vision: When the promised Messiah came, the people of God would "repair the ruined cities, the devastations of many generations" (Isa.61: 4 RSV). The Messiah came, conquered sin and death, and began the process of restoration. The church, as the continuing incarnation of Christ in the world, has a messianic role to play in fulfilling the ancient vision. God is making His appeal through us (II Corinthians 5:20). Our mission is to cooperate with what God is doing in the world until the kingdom is fully come.

In the intensity of their personal needs and generational devastations, the city is a strategic place for the coming kingdom. Inner city ministry the modern day ("by ways") is the front line in the battle for the city's restoration and peace. In this manuscript my objective is to explore why our modern day churches are not effective in reaching the modern day "byways" and offer solutions as a beginning to understanding the mission of the church to the inner city. My interest in this subject is the result of fifteen years of urban evangelism and pastoral ministry. Additionally, I've spent the past three years planting and nurturing a ministry deep within the inner city of West Palm Beach, Florida. The section of West Palm Beach metropolitan area that I serve is called Riviera Beach. It is considered the center of drug sales and abuse, prostitution, child abuse, social and economic impoverishment. As I labor in the field of the inner city I sense a spiritual paradigm shift in the body of Christ. God is raising up a generation of compassionate individuals, lay-leaders, and pastors who are committed to taking the gospel to the streets, by all means necessary. They are becoming all things to all people as one writer says it, "that they may save some!"

I also see amidst this shift, the institutionalized church living in denial of the changes now taking place, or they are escaping into a fear-based bunker mentality in response to it. Like it or not the "glory cloud" is moving again. God is leading us to the inner cities and is raising up His "Byways Church." The pointed steeples and the stained glass windows of our past will not identify this church. Somehow I think we lost our vision of the kingdom under the steeple and behind the stained glass windows. The "Byways Church" will be what Christ actually had in mind, a church that is alive and vibrant in each and every believer's heart. You will be able to identify it not by the glistening exterior of a building, but by the fervent compassion that will flow from one individual of humanity to another. This identification, which will mark the true church, will ask nothing in return except that which is only essential to the vision of advancing the Kingdom of God in the earth.

The renowned African American Poet, Maya Angelou, expressed the dearth of spiritual healing and identification in the traditional church of our day. In her book of poetry, *I Shall Not Be Moved*, Ms. Angelou paints a vivid portrait of our dilemma in the following poem: [2]

<u>*Savior*</u>

Petulant priests, greedy
centurions, and one million
incensed gestures stand
between your love and me.

Your agape sacrifice
is reduced to colored glass,
vapid penance, and the tedium of ritual.

Your footprints yet
mark the crest of billowing seas but
your joy
fades upon the tablets
of ordained prophets.

Visit us again, Savior.

Introduction

> Your children, burdened with
> disbelief, blinded by a patina
> of wisdom,
> carom down this vale of
> fear. We cry for you
> although we have lost
> your name.

Endnotes

[1] Williams, Preston, "Urban Evangelism: A Call for Compassion" (<u>Church of God Evangel</u>, 1991), p. 12.

[2] Angelou, Maya, *I Shall Not Be Moved* (New York: Random House, 1990), p. 30.

CHAPTER ONE

Cheap Talk, No Labor

The Modern Church: A Fortress of Exclusion (Prejudice) or A Fortress of Inclusion (Hope)

In my introduction I spoke of a ministry paradigm shift. Those still thinking and performing ministry in 19th and 20th century paradigms are fossilizing at this moment. I believe we are on the verge of a post-modern Great Awakening—a tremendous historical moment and movement of the Holy Spirit. This 19th and 20th century thinking involved a segregated church, believing that certain cultures belonged within their own socio-economic classes. I concur with Watchman Nee's depiction of the partial dilemma of the church being discrimination. He targets the large cosmopolitan cities of the world saying: "…there are churches for the whites and churches for the blacks, churches for the Europeans and churches for the Asiatics (and now churches for the economically challenged). These have originated through failure to understand that the boundary of a church is a city. God does not permit any division of His children on the ground of differences of color, custom, or manner of living."[1]

We as the body of Christ should be able to transcend all

external differences so that we might in one church show forth the unified life and oneness of the Spirit of His Son. But the description of the church of the Lord Jesus Christ has been redefined more by human intolerance than by the original divine blueprints. This redefining caused a "dividing asunder" of our identity of oneness in God. This caused the birthing of denominations, which I refer to as "different slices of the whole." One denominational slice builds a doctrine around a particular theological thought and condemns the other denominational slices who have done the same thing but in another area of scripture that fit their desire to express religion. From this we find each embracing their unique slice rather than discerning the whole and coming into the unity of the faith. It's no surprise that those who occupy the inner city (believers and nonbelievers alike) don't really know much about the church's mission or its identity. The church itself has a blindsided view of its identity. Identity is the essential catalyst of hope. It breeds definition and creates an atmosphere of belonging, which inspires hope to those who have no hope.

For a moment, lets take a closer look at a common misconception concerning the church. No perception is more firmly rooted in our culture (modern, post-modern) than that the church is a building. This is a view held by both churched and unchurched. We call the place where we worship, *the church*. When we say we are "building a church," it usually means we are constructing a facility, not that we are building men and women in spiritual maturity. This is no harmless colloquialism. It both presupposes and conditions our view of the church, creating what some have aptly called the "edifice complex," wherein the importance and success of the church is directly measured by the size, and grandeur of the structure. Now this may seem trivial to some but look at the underlying problem and the seed misdirection. The grandeur of the structure and its magnificence will begin to spawn certain status ideologies about the mission of the church, its evangelistic target groups, and the maintenance of community reputation. Maintaining the social status of the so-called "church" will become the mission of this "church."

Their interest for the inner city (the byways) consists simply in donations to keep "these people" clothed, fed (physically), and sheltered... in their own surrounding of course. What happens if these individuals desire to know the God that *they* worship, hoping that they too can experience the transforming effects of the gospel? Many within my inner city congregation have shared with me one horror story after another of their rejection while attempting to find solace and hope in the "modern church." Some have communicated that they were politely escorted out of the church facility because of their attire. Some were allowed in the sanctuary but seated in the rear or off to the side tucked away from immediate view. A group of men from a Christian addiction recovery center attended a local congregation one Sunday morning with their director. As they entered the church facilities they were immediately held suspect and were snubbed by parishioners. Women clutched their purses for dear life, assuming the impossibility of such persons attending a worship service for the hope of overcoming life's challenges.

At that time I had accepted the director's invitation to conduct a Tuesday night Bible study at the recovery center. I only committed for six weeks because of the increase of my evangelistic schedule. It was during this time that God gave me a ministry vision for the inner city. Six weeks turned into six months and six months to a year. Finally, I cancelled my evangelistic meetings and yielded to the call of God to plant a "Byways" church. Not only has the community harvest responded, today that entire addiction recovery ministry has been submitted under my ministry for spiritual covering. These men have turned out to be some of the best individuals I've had the opportunity to work with in my 21 years of ministry. I found out that many have experienced the same "status prejudice." What is needed in our day is a renewal of minds in the body of Christ. We're witnessing an era in church history where judgment must begin with the people of God. If the church is going to be triumphant we must become universal in our reach without discrimination.

It is in a triumphant, universal church that the true character and nature of Christ will be expressed. The true character and nature of Christ can be summed up in one word, LOVE. Mother Teresa has this to say about the void in humanity: "Being unwanted is the disease of all. This is the poverty we find around us here. The hunger is not so much for bread and rice but to be loved, to be someone."[2] Only those who are humble can show love. I'm not referring to the worldly kind of love that is counterfeit and object-oriented. That kind of love seeks only to get and not to give. Biblical love is not like that. It's not an emotion; it is an act of sacrificial service. It's not an attitude; it's an action. Love always *does* something. The words used to describe love in 1 Corinthians 13:4-7 are all verbs. Love is an act of service that flows from a heart of humility. In essence, Biblical love meets people's needs. The body of Christ should emulate Jesus' love example in responding to the needs of people.

Jesus' love caused Him to go directly to the people, to love and affirm them. Because they trusted Him, many came to believe in Him. Jesus' method of ministering to people around their needs offers us a powerful example. Jesus met the Samaritan woman around her deepest felt need (having her dignity affirmed), loved her around that need (by starting an unheard-of dialogue), made her need his very own (asking for a drink), then shared with her the "wonderful plan" by helping her discover her deeper need. There is an old Chinese poem that illustrates the felt-need concept very clearly:

Cheap Talk, No Labor

> *Go to the people*
> *Live among them*
> *Learn from them*
> *Love them*
> *Start with what you know*
> *Build on what they have:*
> *But of the best leaders*
> *When their task is done*
> *The people will remark*
> *"We have done it ourselves."* [3]

If we don't grasp the intrinsically corporate nature of Christianity embodied in the church, we are missing the very heart of Jesus' plan. Christopher Dawson made a statement that sums up my thoughts on the Modern day church and it's mindset... "Every Christian mind is a seed of change so long as it is a living mind, not enervated by custom or ossified by prejudice. A Christian has only ***to be*** in order to change the world, for in that act of being, is contained all the mystery of supernatural life. It is the function of the church to sow this Divine seed, to produce not merely good men, but spiritual men—that is to say, super men. In so far as the church fulfills this function it transmits to the world a continuous stream of spiritual energy. If the salt loses its savor, then indeed the world sinks back into disorder and death."[4]

Connect The Dots
(Melding A Fragmented Social Structure)

Charles Colson shares a very interesting story, which I believe, presents a perfect example of how to connect the dots of this fragmented social structure within the body of Christ. His friend and mentor, Richard Halverson, is chaplain of the U.S. Senate. Before his senate service he was pastor of Washington D.C.'s large Fourth Presbyterian Church. He had been pastoring Fourth Presbyterian for years, when suddenly, Dick (Richard) says, he saw his church clearly for the very first time. He was flying into Washington one day at dusk. Since the approach path to Washington's National Airport happened to pass directly over Fourth Presbyterian Church, Dick pressed his face against the window to catch a glimpse of the building from the air. But everything on the ground was shrouded in the shadows falling over the city as the sun set. Dick could not find his church.

He leaned back in his seat, watching the fast-approaching Washington skyline, always an inspiring sight. As his eyes followed the Potomac River, Dick could see the skyscrapers of Rosslyn, just across Key Bridge from Georgetown. Then, in the distance to the left, the White House, the lights of the Labor Department, the distant glow of the Capitol dome. As he stared out the window, he began mentally ticking off the names of members of his congregation who worked in those office buildings and government bureaus. Disciples he had equipped to live their faith. And suddenly it hit him. "Of course!" he exclaimed to the startled passenger in the next seat. "There it is! Fourth Presbyterian Church!" The church wasn't marked by a sanctuary or a steeple. The church was spread throughout Washington, in the homes and neighborhoods and offices below him, thousands of points of light illuminating the darkness. And that is the way the church should look in the world today. The people of God—one body with many different parts—spread throughout every arena of life, twenty-four hours a day, seven days a week, doing even "greater things" than Christ Himself![5]

The "byways" are a very important part of that "big picture." I believe that the body of Christ would do well to get a vision of the inner city (the modern day byways) from the position of God who sits on high and looks low. To connect the dots of this socio-spiritual fragmentation will require the church to stretch. The church that seeks, surveys, and reaches out beyond their comfort zones will quickly learn how others view the church. It may be threatening at first, but it can become a powerful positive catalyst for change. You see, that is what I had to come to terms with. Coming from a main line denomination, I was too blinded by sectarian doctrines, political aspirations, contribution goals, membership drives, and sermon quotas to discern how the world viewed most churches. They viewed us as being more concerned about social image and building programs than people. In essence, the church was not concerned about what they could do for the masses but instead, what the masses could do for them and their organizational reputation.

The twenty-first century church must make paradigm shifts in the way we look at and understand our culture and the mission of the church. America (especially the inner city) is spiritually thirsty. They are hungry for hope. They are examining the world's smorgasbord of spiritual offerings, looking for someone… something to be as hungry and thirsty, to be the catalyst for meeting their needs as they are of getting their needs met. After decades of advancing secularism, oppressive communism, and declining spiritual interest, a spiritual awakening is sweeping the world and the inner city is right in the middle of it. It is important to note that spiritual interest does not necessarily mean an interest in Christianity or the church. People want to experience the supernatural. They want to feel God, and they are looking everywhere. If the church of Jesus Christ doesn't recognize the diamonds in the rough of the inner city, some other ungodly influence will. Whoever offers them a solution to their problem (godly or not) they will jump. It has been said that if you offer a thirsty man in a desert a glass of sand he would drink it!

The inner city is no different, they are thirsty, and they've been rejected by both the modern church and society.

They're reaching. They are looking for a place where they can meet God, experience the power of the Holy Spirit, and where their lives can be radically changed. We have a generation that is less interested in cerebral arguments, linear thinking, theological systems, and more interested in encountering the supernatural. Now that we know this, the twenty-first century church must not be preoccupied with internal issues, petty conflicts, and traditional divisions. Those are all luxuries of affluence and of a religious culture (akin to the order of the Pharisees and Sadducee). In an increasingly secular culture, we must have the wherewithal to lead seekers to an authentic encounter with God, or they will look somewhere else.

If churches are going to be effective we must become flexible and creative in our approach to ministry. We live in different times. In this respect Leith Anderson shares a simple yet profound reflection of the New Testament churches and their tone of ministry. He says that, "While the New Testament speaks often about churches, it is surprisingly silent about many matters that we associate with church structure and life. There is no mention of architecture, pulpits, lengths of typical sermons, or rules for having a Sunday school. Little is said about style of music, order of worship, or times of church gatherings. There were no Bibles, denominations, camps, pastors conferences, or board meeting minutes." He continues by saying, "Those who strive to be New Testament churches must seek to live out its principles not reproduce its details. We don't know many of the details, and if we reproduced the ones we know, we would end up with synagogues, speaking Greek, and the divisive sins of the Corinthians."

Anderson goes on, "Each church in the first century had its own personality and style, fitted to its time and place. The Ephesian church was not a franchise of the Jerusalem church. Change and creativity were welcomed."[6] I firmly believe that if we're going to reach the inner city a new engagement of ministry is essential. This does not require any deviations from the Bible, but it does require the freedom to respond to the creativity of the Spirit. Without any doubt, this will shake up any traditional foundations that are not conducive to reaching 21st century souls. The major cause for rejecting "byway" souls is that they represent change, traditional reevaluation, and the introduction of a balanced social / ministry playing field where everyone is accepted no matter what their socio-economic status. Scary isn't it? Only to those who thrive on sitting at the modern day high seats in the temple and those who enjoy being hailed as they procession down the highways of their great cities on their way to their great churches, never thinking twice about their brothers and sister who watch them pass *by the way* on the other side (remember the story of the "Good Samaritan").

Endnotes

[1] Nee, Watchman, *The Normal Christian Church Life*, (Anaheim, CA: Living Stream Ministry, 1980), p. 92.

[2] Commencement speech at Harvard University, 1982.

[3] Perkins, M. John, *Beyond Charity*, (Grand Rapid, MI: Baker Books, 1993), p. 35.

[4] Dawson, Christopher, *Christianity and the New Age*, (Manchester, N.H.: Sophia Institute, 1985), p. 2.

[5] Colson, Charles, *The Body: Being Light In The Darkness*, (Dallas, TX: Word Publishing, 1992), p. 271, 272.

[6] Anderson, Leith, *A Church For The 21st Century*, (Minneapolis, MN: Bethany House, 1992), p. 62.

CHAPTER TWO

Restoring Dashed Dreams

"I'm Ok, You're Ok?"

In 1973, author, Thomas A. Harris, published a book entitled "*I'm Ok, You're Ok.*" I purposely included a question mark at the end of my subtopic, because that is not always the case. This seems to be the general attitude with most suburbanites. They don't face the devastating issues that are confronting the inner city underclass each day. So for them, it is easy to over look the problems, the needs, and the emotional hunger in the lives of the masses. The suburbanites assume that if *I'm ok, then you're ok*. This is far from the truth. Something happened on September 11, 2001 that shook and shocked America. The massive destruction of New York's World Trade Center and the partial destruction of the Pentagon in Washington, D.C. at the hands of terrorists is a sad but potent example of my point. Without indulging the horrific details, the point I'd like to extract from this tragedy is the fact that terrorism has always been around but most American citizens have overlooked it. We have not been as sensitive and sympathetic to the hurt that it causes in the lives of others, until now.

I witnessed a change in the nations' attitude, emotional well being, and financial stability or the lack there of. Because terrorism had hit the homeland, there is now an interest in stamping out this atrocity on a global scale. My question is, "Why wasn't America as involved in the fight against terrorism before this atrocity?" Could it be that the rest of the world was, metaphorically speaking, a "byway" in the sight of the America? Is it possible that what has happened on a larger scale in New York and Washington, D.C. is the exact same thing we're dealing with in our major cities around the nation? If we can, but for a moment, imagine that this analogy is real; will it take the "byways" of our major cities exploding emotionally and entering into the suburbs to bring attention to the anguish and hurt that permeates the inner cities daily? Hear the words of Jeremiah who had a haunting indictment for priests and prophets in Israel:

> *"They dress the wound of my people*
> *As though it were not serious.*
> *'Peace, peace,' they say,*
> *when there is no peace."*
> *(Jeremiah 8:11)*

Even during Jeremiah's time it is as if the people were saying, "I'm ok, you're ok." But the reality is that things are not ok. It is only an illusion to those who chose to close their eyes to the truth that surrounds them daily. It is time for us to prove that the purpose of the gospel is to reconcile alienated people to God and to each other, across racial, cultural, social, and economic barriers.

There have been countless documentaries (both on television and in publications) featuring the issue of, as the media describes, the underclass or inner city dwellers. I have ministered and walked among them for the past two years.

Much of what I am writing reflects my own experience with them. I have found that it is one thing to be exposed to the stories of America's inner city dilemma, but quite another thing to experience it first hand. For the sake of embracing how these individuals view themselves, I will use the term "underclass" throughout this chapter and refer to it from time to time throughout this book.

Research reveals that consistently, thirty million plus Americans fall below the official poverty line. Of this group, there is a subculture of ten million or more who are not just economically poor but who remain stuck at the bottom of the social ladder. This non-working, unassimilated, hard-to-reach marginal class is centered in cities and is referred to by different names: the downtrodden, the underprivileged, the disadvantaged, the down-and-out, outcasts, or simply the "underclass." This kind of stereotyping is common and extremely destructive. It imparts a sense of worthlessness and a feeling of insignificance. It's no wonder that America's hard-core poor have succumbed to hostility and helplessness, to feelings of being out of control and unable to advance. I see this in the faces of these individuals week in and week out. They are economically poor, but what concerns me most is that they are emotionally impoverished as well. In their world things are not "ok" and as a result, they live in a "not so ok" mindset.

Counseling with them exposes me to a long history of child abuse, traumatized alcoholics and drug addicts, the chronically homeless, ex-convicts and youth offenders, illiterate school dropouts, and released mental patients. The underclass also includes violent gang members, male and female prostitutes, and street criminals who may or may not be economically poor. They are composed of people from all strata of society who lack the education, personal discipline, and motivation needed to be effective and valuable in the world of work and responsible living. They just can't seem to pull it all together because they just don't know how. The "byway" is a place where no one cares, a place where no one bothers to teach them, and a place where proper role models are few and far between. For them, things are not "ok."

It is at this pivotal point within the inner city that the "sons and daughters of God" must come forth and show them what belongs to them and their future. If we can challenge them to see their surroundings as God envisions it they could breathe life into what the suburbanites consider a wasteland. Consider the story of Abraham, Sarah, and Lot. A dispute arose between Abraham and Lot's herdsmen over the division of land. Abraham, trusting in his vision, suggested that they part company: "If you go to the left, I'll go to the right; if you go to the right, I'll go to the left."

Lot looked east and "saw that the whole plain of the Jordan was well watered, like the garden of the Lord, like the land of Egypt." Based on immediate appearances, Lot chose for himself the lush Jordan plain and settled near Sodom. Abraham was left with the hilly country of Canaan that did not seem as pleasing to the eye. It was at the point of departure that God confirmed Abraham's vision: "Lift up your eyes from where you are and look north and south, east and west. All the land that you see I will give you and your offspring forever" (Genesis 13:9-10. 14-15). There is a lesson here for today's inner city visionaries: *The eyes of faith do not focus on appearances but look up and visualize what can be.* "What you can see beyond the immediate, I can give you," God is saying to people of faith. "What you cannot envision, I cannot give you."[1] Faith to look beyond what they know and see is what is needed. We must motivate them to become dreamers.

Dr. Paul Yongi Cho expresses it this way, "Show me your dreams, and I will show you your future." This is a powerful saying! In Jesus Christ we find our ability to dream, to tap into that realm that is reserved for the called out of God.

It is here that those who are found amidst the "byways" will find, as Jesus so profoundly states, "the things that belong to your peace." Patience and waiting on God is the key to their deliverance. The inner cities did not get like this over night and dreams were not destroyed in a day. Likewise, we must encourage them to pace their forward movement and acknowledge the progressive hand of God day by day. The following is a poetic piece later put to music, which I think, projects the proper spirit of the new dreamer:

> If you want your dream to be,
> Take your time, go slowly.
> Do few things but do them well.
> Heartfelt work grows purely.
>
> Day by day, stone by stone,
> Build your secrets slowly.
> Day by day, you'll grow too,
> You'll know heaven's glory.
>
> If you want to live free,
> Take your time, go slowly.
> Do few things but do them well,
> Heartfelt joys are holy.[2]

I continually seek God's wisdom as I counsel those in the byways. I know all to well how easy it is to get caught up in dreaming and encouraging others to dream without understanding proper "pace." The "tyranny of the urgent" rushes in and the pace accelerates. The results will be a crisis management ministry: never-ending demands. Overwhelming needs, too little money, everyone spread too thin, resulting in staff burnout. I recently conducted a leadership "reasoning session." This was a session where those assisting me in ministry have the opportunity to share their frustrations concerning themselves and their position of service. A young lady who served as our Children's Ministry Director shared that she was so excited about our vision for the inner city and that she accepted the position with heightened enthusiasm and many goals for accomplishing what she thought God had placed in her heart. Well, as she expressed her frustration, it was apparent that she was facing burnout, to the point of "dropout."

The point is, as we begin to empower individuals to become "dreamers," we must also teach them the importance of pace and process. The intensity and challenge of change threatens to destroy even the most confident visionary. They must know that the way to "live life free to dream" is to let your vision unfold slowly, "day by day, step by step," following the rhythm of the Spirit.

"Dust Off Your Dreams"

Helping individuals to dust off their dreams, realize their potential and identify their significance to the kingdom of God is an enormous task. As you have read, the inner city way of living is quite different from the suburbanite. Christians have been called to do the Lord's work in the Lord's way. Recognizing that privilege ought to thrill us. Do you realize that the Almighty God, the ruler of heaven and earth, has said, "Would you be My personal envoy, taking My message to people for as long as you live?" William Barclay has correctly said, "It is not the man who glorifies the work but the work which glorifies the man. There is no dignity like the dignity of a great task."[3] The greatest tasks of dusting off dreams along the "byways" is getting individuals to understand that their perception of themselves is in direct contrast with God's perception of them. This is a prerequisite to dreaming, to becoming a visionary.

As a dreamer they will discover who they really are, they will learn that their purpose, their identity, their uniqueness and their potential are interdependent. It is said by one Greek philosopher to "know thyself," but you cannot truly know your self until you discover your purpose. The key to reaching one's full potential in God is to renounce negative thoughts about His wonderful and glorious creation... you! Dr. I.V. Hilliard in his book, *Mental Toughness for Success*, expresses a wonderful aspect of preparing one's self to receive God's a revelation of their "true" self. He said, "We must seek deliverance from inferior thought patterns. The most important choice that you and I could ever make is the choice to become a born-again Christian. But here is an undeniable fact, when we become a born-again Christian we bring our old inferior thought patterns into the Kingdom of God. This for the most part, is contrary to the teaching of Godly principles." He goes on to say, "A mind that is void of the control of the ministry of the Holy Spirit is incapable of correctly directing your life."[4]

As we teach them to yield their mind to the transforming power of the Word and the Holy Spirit of God, we will begin to see lives transformed, dreams and visions manifesting, neighborhoods changing, and the world will stand back in wonderment. Dreaming, I believe, is a way that God allows individuals to take the small steps toward His larger purpose for their lives. Once purpose is known then the particular components God built into the individual will enable him or her to achieve all that He has prepared for them. Dreaming gives humanity the opportunity to participate in initiating the divine plan for life. In essence, it is important for the hopeless, the downtrodden, and the one caught in the matrix of despair to understand that purpose does not just happen as a by-product of life. They are responsible for the intentional fulfillment of their dreams so that their world (inner city / byways) may benefit from their contribution and that the Kingdom of Heaven is advanced, magnifying the glory of God in the earth.

Thomas A. Bruno, author of *Take Your Dreams and Run* said, "To deny your dreams is to deny your destiny." Bruno additionally cites Woodrow Wilson saying, "We grow great by dreams. All big men are dreamers. They see things in the soft haze of a spring day, or in the fire on a long winter's evening. Some of us let these great dreams die, but others nourish them and protect them through bad days, till they bring them to the sunshine and light which comes always to those who sincerely hope that dreams will come true."[5] I have embraced this quote as a power nugget in my life and have shared it with many in my ministry. It represents hope without any false illusions. Part of my mission is to inspire others to dream. It is God who defines purpose, which He has revealed to us within our innate nature, through dreams and visions. Yet, we must be quick to also echo the fact that the road to the fulfillment of dreams is not obstacle free nor is it a popular way.

The only thing the well-paved path tells you is which way the crowd is moving. Most "byway" individuals have been following the crowds all of their lives and it is this mindset that the negative state of their status in life is nurtured. They have followed the wrong crowds down the wrong roads in life. Robert Frost, the American poet (1874-1963), gave the world this simple yet profound truth, "Two roads diverged in the woods, and I took the one less traveled, and that has made all the difference." As I ride through the inner city streets of West Palm Beach and Riviera Beach, I encounter the masses that chose to take the familiar paths of life. The paths of those who traveled this same road before them are filled with wasted, disoriented lives of individuals who had dreams, desires, plans, and aspirations. They are lost in a maze of substance abuse, and alcoholism; covered under the crusted rock of experience without covenant. Under covenant, God has promised that "...all things (good or bad) work together for your good, to them who are under covenant, for them who are called according to His purpose" (Romans 8:28). I'm reminded of a story concerning Michelangelo. A visitor interrupted him in his studio and asked, "what he was doing." At that time, the great artist had just received a magnificent piece of marble. He began at once, chiseling one of the corners, working at what appeared to be a wing. Listen to his answer to the visitor, "There is an angel imprisoned within the marble and I am trying to set him free." Within the marble was the imagination of a dream. Locked within the hearts of every "byway" individual is that dreamer with only the tip of its wing showing. It is time the body of Christ came to the forefront, out of the "I'm ok" world of suburbia and put their hands to the "task plow" of setting them free! God has made a part of them that wants to dream, a part of them that is not subjected to the statistics of society that all too often discourage and dash their dreams.

Endnotes

[1] Christensen, Michael J., *City Streets City People*, (Nashville, TN: Abingdon Press, 1988), p. 55.

[2] Leitch, Donovan, *Little Church*, (Famous Music Corporation, 1973).

[3] Barclay, William, *The Letter to the Corinthians*, (Philadelphia: Westminster, 1975), p. 165.

[4] Hilliard, I.V., *Mental Toughness for Success*, (Houston: Light, 1996), p. 40.

[5] Bruno, Thomas A., *Take Your Dreams and Run*, (South Plainfield: Bridge, 1984), p. 2-3.

CHAPTER THREE

Healing Inner Conflict

Counseling: The Integration of Psychology and Spirituality

After salvation then what? As with all humanity, the "byway" souls have many issues to contend with. Pastors who minister within the inner city will need to rethink their approach to resolving personal struggles of these lost souls. What I have found in my experience with other ministries in the inner city are pastors who have little or no educational training (theology, psychology, counseling, ect.). What I am hearing is the old familiar cliché, "All I need is the anointing of God." While I agree that the call and anointing of God are definitely essential for successful ministry, I also have a firm conviction that to prepare one's self for the destiny and purpose appointed to you is key to our effectiveness. Paul, the apostle, even admonishes us to "study to show ourselves approved before God, a workman that will not be ashamed" (2 Timothy 2:15). There is another reason; lost souls are depending on your being properly trained. After salvation Paul contends that we should "renew our minds." The renewing of the mind involves several aspects, but I'd like to focus on two: (1) The Rightly Divided Word, and (2) Proper Counseling.

I will deal with the first focus of this "renewing" process in the latter part of this chapter. Counseling is a very important part of any ministry, but more so in the "byway" ministry. Most of these individuals were reared with little or no discipline, serious family dysfunctions, and a not so pleasant environment to say the least. The pastor or minister to the inner city will face incest victims, rapes, murderers, single parents in distress, drug dealers, users, and prostitutes. The list goes on and on, sometimes it seems as if there is no end to the atrocity. After salvation, these individuals need help resolving past issues in their lives. This is where the trained minister becomes most effective in the life of the redeemed soul.

With the average person, coming to terms with the truth about themselves produces emotional pain (anxiety, guilt, and fear). This effect is doubled and sometimes squared for those living in the inner city. After the experience of salvation many habitually and continually deceive themselves to maintain a false sense of self-esteem and to alleviate emotional pain. Christian counseling is of the utmost importance in the inner city. For them, the effect of spiritual depravity runs deeper than most. They live in a potent "stronghold" environment and are open to the wickedness of the worst influences. A change of heart and mind is needed. When referring to the heart and mind, you are dealing with the redirecting of passion and thought. Vance Havner once said, " You cannot change a man's heart, but you can change his mind and when man changes his mind, God will then change his heart." Our objective in counseling should be to assist in the renewing of one's mind, the discipline of thought, and clear perception.

I believe the key to understanding Christian psychology is found in Jeremiah 17:9: "The heart is deceitful above all things, and desperately wicked: who can know it?" When reading this it is obvious that man is blind to his own sinfulness. Solomon, who could have had any wish he wanted from God, chose God's wisdom and insight into human nature, so he could judge his people well. This gifting is certainly essential in the counseling ministry. After counseling and judging thousands of people, Solomon said that, "with much wisdom comes much sorrow; the more knowledge, the more grief" (Ecclesiastes 1:18). Frank B. Minirth & Paul D. Meier expanded on this verse of scripture saying, "Finding out the truth about human depravity is a painful process that brings temporary grief, partly because the more we learn about the depraved motives, desires, and defense mechanisms of humankind in general, the more we learn about our own. In the end, that knowledge and its remedy can bring us joy and a greater acceptance of others." [1]

It wasn't until I began my inner city ministry and counseled on a weekly basis that I understood the depth of God's grace. I relate more now to Paul's counsel to the church at Rome when he said, "...where sin abounded, grace did much more abound" (Romans 5:20). Inner city counseling ministered to my life as much as it did to those with whom I was counseling. I was able to connect with their many hurts and frustrations. In general the word *counsel* refers to advice given as a result of consultation. Although different schools of psychological thought vary greatly in their methodology, the actual intent of counseling is nearly always the same, namely, to assist someone (who has asked for help) in dealing with a problem. Before studying psychology I found myself using some of the basic counseling methodologies. The inner city individual is one who is, on the exterior and at times internally, tough. They have to be, it is their way of life, it is survival. When he or she comes into a counseling session you will have to chisel through many layers of defense mechanisms to expose the root of their issues.

The Bible uses several words for counsel. From the Old Testament to the New Testament we find slightly varying definitions. The following are just a few examples. In them, we will find that they imply that different approaches are suitable for different situations. You will need them all working with inner city ministry. In the New Testament there are a number of Greek words pertaining to counsel. Five of them can be found in 1 Thessalonians 5:14:

1. *Parakaleo* – to beseech, exhort, encourage, comfort (Rom. 12:1; 15:30; 2 Cor. 1:4; 1 Thess. 5:11).
2. *Noutheteo* – to put in mind, warn, confront (Rom. 15:14; 1 Cor. 4:14; Col. 3:16).
3. *Paramutheomai* – to cheer up, encourage (1 Thess. 2:11; John 11:19,31).
4. *Antechomai* – to cling to, to hold fast to, to take an interest in (Matt. 6:24; Luke 16:13).
5. *Makrothumeo* – to be patient (Matt. 18:26, 29; Heb. 6:15; James 5:7).

Moreover, in the Old Testament there are several Hebrew words pertaining to counsel:

1. *ya'ats* – A general term to advise, counsel, consult. Used approximately eighty times in the Old Testament, with the first use describing Jethro's counsel to Moses (Exod. 18:19).
2. *dabar* – the "counsel of Balaam" (Num. 31:6) refer to advice.
3. *sowd* – David's reference to the "sweet counsel" (Ps. 55:14, KJV) he had received from a former friend carries the connotation of fellowship and sharing.
4. *eta* – that Daniel answered Arioch "with counsel" (Dan. 2:14, KJV) implies that he responded with discretion.
5. *etsah* – Israel's lack "in counsel" (Deut. 32:28) sug-

gests a lack of understanding.
6. *yasad* – "the rulers take counsel together" (Ps. 2:2) means that they sit down together for a period of mutual consultation, deliberation, and instruction.[2]

I thought it necessary to share the above references to show how important counsel was before the establishment of the Church and after its birth after the outpouring of the Spirit of God on the Day of Pentecost. In reading over these, it is imperative that we notice five of the main approaches found in modern psychology.

Methodology: Ways to Counsel
1. *Listening.* By simply listening the counselor can help the counselee unburden himself of deep-seated hurts and to begin to feel understood. Elihu (Job 32) was a good listener. The one indictment inner city individuals have against ministries and suburbanites is that they think no one is listening, which in their minds, equates to not caring.
2. *Self-disclosure.* The counselor may wish to share personal examples from his own life (if they will help rather than hinder the counselee). The apostle Paul used this technique (2 Corinthians). To hear that they are not the only one who have problems or have come face to face with despair will assist in opening the reluctant heart of one who have so many layers of defense mechanisms to work through. Inner city dwellers are convinced that no one understands what they are going through and are therefore quite resentful at first. But honesty about your own struggles would make a world of difference in sessions when needed.
3. *Directives.* Straightforward, direct advice is often beneficial. Christ frequently used this approach as did Solomon (Proverbs). If you've ever had the opportu-

nity to minister in the inner city you will readily concur with me when I say that this is an imperative in counseling. You're engaging in communications with individuals who are street smart and have the savvy of survival, they can handle straight talk. In fact, they are offended when you're not straight with them. They perceive it as a con. Of course discretion and timing is imperative at this juncture. Be led by the Spirit.
4. *Indirect Techniques.* Stories, parables, and questions can be used to help a person gain insight. Christ often taught others by asking them questions or telling parables (Matt. 13). This is a very effective tool for me in the inner city. Because the education level and tolerance is low, I used these techniques in both my teaching and counseling sessions. In fact, I consider my teaching session as a counseling session from God's Word.
5. *Combination of Directives and Indirect Techniques.* Drs. Minirth & Meier shared that they often begin by using indirect techniques to help the counselee gain insight into himself; then they give direct advice based on the Bible as absolute standard. In the Old Testament Nathan used a story to help David discern the nature of his sin, then confronted him (2 Sam.12).

Christian counseling is more complex than other forms of counseling because our goals are multifaceted. Whereas the behaviorist can focus on symptom reduction and the psychoanalyst on ego strength, Christian counselors are concerned with spiritual growth as well as mental health. As we turn our attention to the next subtopic, *The Word: Modern Day Manna*, in the process of healing inner conflict, I'd like to reference the insight of Malcolm A. Jeeves. In his book, Human Nature at the Millennium, he connects the dots that separate psychology, philosophy, and theology.

Jeeves advocates that the proper counseling approach enables us to build up a substantial composite picture of the mechanisms that may be at work, in the moment-by-moment, ongoing activity of human beings, as they take information from their environment, process it, store it, and as appropriate, act on it. He also notes that there is an altogether different stream of knowledge about human nature that comes to us from the writings of wise men down through the centuries, such as the remarkable insights of great writers like Shakespeare, and these also provide enduring insights into our human nature, as do the insights of philosophers, poets, artists, and others. This stream of information for the Christian, is subordinate to a source of knowledge and information about human nature that takes primacy over all else; this is the knowledge given to us by God through revelation in Scripture and above all in the person of Jesus Christ. The Bible is full of profound insights into human nature and teaches us how God would have us live our lives day by day, individually, in social interactions with others, and above all, in relationship with Him.[3]

The Word: Modern Day Manna in Counseling

When I look over the harvest of the inner city I see hungry, wandering individuals such as we see in the exodus of Israel from Egypt. They are in the wilderness of the major cities and are in need of the daily provisions God has promised. Manna was the divine nutrient for those who assembled in the wilderness and the Word of God is the modern day nutrient. Not only is it a nutrient, but it is also a guide to spiritual and emotional well-being. Mark McMinn refers to it as a map. He says that we need a map for spiritual growth. This map must be true to Scripture and theologically sound yet completely relevant to the various mental health problems we see. Furthermore, it must be a practical map, not one of those complex figures that can be understood only by philosophers and theologians and has limited use in the counseling office. And ideally it should be a map that leads us beyond the standard theoretical commitments to behavioral, cognitive, psychodynamic, family systems, and other forms of therapy. We want a deeper understanding of the spiritual life and spiritual wisdom that will allow us to see our clients, our counseling relationships, and ourselves more accurately. Finally, it should be a map that assumes neither a one-to-one correspondence between spiritual and psychological health nor complete separation between the two.[4] In essence, it should bring us to a full integration of therapies that will bring wholeness to our clients.

This scriptural map centers on exegesis, the meditation of Scripture that centers on internalizing and personalizing the passage. This is the power of the Word in counseling. The written Word becomes a living word addressed to the reader. When I assist an individual to matriculate into this realm, I witness a life-changing phenomenon. When we counsel with the Word as our road map, it will introduce the counselee to their true identity. It has been said that people cannot consistently behave in a manner inconsistent with their self-perception. If we consider ourselves losers, and call ourselves alcoholics, these pronouncements can become self-fulfilling prophecies. It is not what we do that determines who we are; it is who we are and how we perceive ourselves that determines what we do.[5]

It is through the Word of God that we ignite a revolution in the thinking of mankind. Scripture plays a crucial role in Christian counseling. By providing spiritual nourishment God's Word produces growth and healing in the counselee. The Christian counselor will employ the Bible with discernment, tact, and sensitivity. There is a variety of ways in which the counselor can use God's Word; for example, as a means of direct challenge and confrontation, or as a source of encouragement and positive reinforcement. The Bible also offers practical advice and numerous examples of godly lives. These are just some of the requisites for successful Christian counseling and how they are relevant to inner city restoration. The wise pastor/counselor will periodically evaluate him or herself and earnestly strive for improvement in those areas where they are falling short.

Scripture has been given by inspiration of God, that the man of God may be perfect (2 Tim. 3:16-17). There is a correlation between strength and the abiding presence of God's Word (1 John 2:14). Perhaps Solomon summed it up best:

My son, give attention to my words;
Incline your ear to my sayings.
Do not let them depart from your sight;
Keep them in the midst of your heart.
For they are life to those who find them,
And health to all their whole body
(Prov. 4:20-22, NASB).

The Christian counselor must be ever on the lookout for different ways and opportunities in which to use the Word of God in counseling. He himself must enjoy the Word, and that enjoyment must be evident to the counselee. Perhaps the greatest need the counselee may have is for someone to communicate to him or her how to find delight in the Word of God. I have found that counseling in the inner city is major ministry. Sixty-five percent of my time is spent in counseling sessions. The need is great but the laborers in this specialized area of counseling are few. I pray daily for the pastors and lay ministers who are working in the "byways." I pray that they will begin to see the need to acquire the skills necessary to properly nurture and shape the precious minds of God's people.

Endnotes

[1] Minirth, Frank B. & Meier, Paul D., *Counseling and The Nature of Man*, (Grand Rapids, MI: Baker, 1982), p. 33.

[2] Minirth 60-61.

[3] Jeeves, Malcolm A., *Human Nature at the Millennium*, (Grand Rapids, MI: Baker, 1997), p. 232.

[4] McMinn, Mark R., *Psychology, Theology, and Spirituality In Christian Counseling*, (Wheaton, IL: Tyndale, 1996), p. 34.

[5] Anderson, Neil T. and Quarles, Mike & Julia, *Freedom From Addiction*, (Ventura, CA: Regal, 1996), p. 232.

CHAPTER FOUR

Preserving The Seed

Breaking Generational Strongholds

"... And there arose another generation after them, which knew not the Lord, nor yet the works which he had done for Israel."
(Judges 2:10b)

When riding through some of the streets in various inner cities, this condition seems to be the heart cry of our day, a generation who doesn't know the Lord. In an era where we've seen changes in our nation that contradict our proclamation of "In God We Trust." An era that further claims "One Nation Under God" but allows prayer to be taken out the schools, subjecting *next generation* souls to learning environments conducive to the onslaught of satanic influences. The seed of generations that are potential Kingdom advancers are at risk. The dearth left by this is felt more so in our inner cities around the nation than anywhere else. I see this predicament as a spiritual epidemic of generation after generation, passing on the strongholds of the past. We see children being groomed for failure because of the lack of proper guidance both spiritual and practical. A vacant seat at the dinner table because the priest of the home is out of place. He has accepted a previous engagement at the table of addiction and despair.

The idea that because my father or mother wasn't able to rise above this condition and dismal plight in life that they are predestined to turn out the same way. The deliverance and preservation of the family seed is of the most important and critical assignments in ministry. We must, as ministers of the Gospel, become Kingdom ambassadors who facilitate the breaking of the generational ties of the past and to assist in the establishment of the Kingdom ties for their future. It is important from the outset of this chapter to speak of precautions concerning generational strongholds, curses, demonic possession, or oppression. These terms are very familiar in this type of study. But as I have studied the areas of psychology and counseling I found that it is essential that a proper diagnosis of the condition be obtained before treatment can be initiated. This is also relative in the arena of spiritual healing and deliverance.

Mickey Bonner gives wise counsel concerning this when involved in spiritual warfare. He says: "The beginning of all cure is the proper diagnosis of the disease. We need to understand that one of the great dangers of a study like this is to begin to see every sin or nervous condition, even fear of sickness, as demonic. There is the natural depravity of man, the activity of the flesh. However, when spirits are involved, one is dealing with flesh out of control."[1]

Bonner uses the terms *demonization* and *flesh out of control* synonymously. For the sake of extended clarity, I have chosen to identify this condition in the same manner as the apostle Paul; who referred to it as *strongholds*. A closer look into the diagnosis of the inner city will reveal some interesting symptoms that become generational baggage for their children and their children's children. No one will disagree with me when I say that the inner city is out of control. This is the same term used by Bonner when he gives a description of the signs that reflect demonization: "Let's look at signs of demonization or flesh out of control.

- Uncontrollable Sin
- No Spiritual Victory
- Abnormal Passions
- Chronic Emotional Turmoil
- Addiction to Alcohol, Nicotine, Sex, Drugs, Vice
- Introspection
- Gluttony
- Nervous and Apprehensive
- Violent Temper
- Instability
- Fear
- Intensely Spiritual[2]

These are the leading strongholds found in the inner city. They represent the "fruit" of the "root," the sin nature of mankind exposed and magnified. Unconfronted and unconfessed sin is the problem. The need for the light of God's Word to illuminate their path is paramount. They need someone to give them the proper diagnosis of their condition and the proper treatment plan, the plan of salvation. Marilyn Hickey says, "We can lay the ax of God's Word to the root of the tree, free ourselves from any generational curse,' and stop it from bearing bad fruit in future generations."[3] We are in an hour when the spiritual hosts of darkness are deploying for what may prove to be some of the most consequential battles of history of the inner city. If we are to emerge from these spiritual encounters triumphantly, we must improve our ability to detect the true circumstances behind the acts of degradation and to identify correctly authentic centers of power.

In reference to this, it is important that I speak, if but briefly, on another aspect of generational strongholds. This aspect involves territorial strongholds. My first objective when entering inner city ministry was to identify and begin interceding against the forces that hover over the city God called me to be an ambassador to. George Otis, Jr., founder and president of The Sentinel Group, a Seattle-based Christian research and information agency, had this to say concerning territorial strongholds: "Almost everyone has had the experience of entering another city, neighborhood or country only to sense an intangible unease or oppression descend upon his or her spirits. In Scripture, certain "spiritual strongmen" (high-ranking spirits) are referred to by the territories they control. These include the prince of Persia (see Dan. 10:13), the prince of Greece (see Dan. 10:20), the king of Tyre (see Ezek. 28:12) and the spirit of Babylon (see Rev. 17:3-5)."[4] C. Peter Wagner, in his book *Wrestling with Dark Angels* (Regal Books), suggests that Satan delegates high-ranking spirits to control nations, regions, cities, tribes, people groups, neighborhoods and other significant social networks. The major assignment of these demonic powers, Wagner believes, "is to prevent God from being glorified in their territory."[5]

Dealing with strongholds, as you see, involves families as well as territories. Expanding the issue further, inner city strongholds are different on many levels than those encountered in the suburbs. Turning the attention back to the inner city predicament, I'd like to share some interesting data that will shed light on the generational strongholds now being faced by those entering "byway" ministries. The inner city, although culturally mixed, is predominately African American. Because this is the case and my inner city experience has been mostly with this culture, I will focus my data on this group. In no way am I excluding the other cultures that make up the minority of the inner city populous. The principles dis-

Preserving The Seed

cussed in this chapter are universal in content and application and is to serve as a mirror to truly see the problem we're facing as well as a catalyst for generational preservation. I have always proclaimed that my ministry purpose is *to win my generation and influence the next.* I would hope that this is the conviction of the body of Christ worldwide.

The Inner city has become synonymous with African Americans. I'm sure this comes as no shock, and by now; you have heard all the statistics:

- Infants born to black teenage girls have a 50 percent higher mortality rate than those of the general population
- 50 percent of black teens are unemployed (triple the rate of whites)
- 25 percent of black men aged 20 through 64 are unemployed
- One-third of blacks live below the poverty line
- 25 percent of black males aged 16 through 30 are in our prison system
- 64 percent of the prison population is black (and yet blacks account for only 12 percent of the general population)
- 600, 000 blacks are in prison, as opposed to 400, 000 in college
- Two-thirds of black children are born to unwed mothers
- 2.6 million of our 4.6 million black families are headed by single women
- Homicide is the leading cause of death for black males aged 15 through 44
- Homicide is the second cause of death for all black males under 70 [6]

When you peruse the statistics, it becomes quite obvious

that we're dealing with generational and territorial strongholds that must be pulled down. Within the fine print of the statistics lie hidden myriads of crushed human spirits and the laughter of those principalities assigned to sift these individual as wheat. Now is the time of salvation, now is the time for the "more than conquerors" to come forth and take back the generations that belong to God.

Establishing Generational Covenants

Establishing generational covenants is an act that I define as "the passing on of the mantle of blessings." It has to do with connectedness in relation to spiritual values. Passing them on from one generation to the next. Rather than enforcing doom and gloom, poverty brainwashing, both spiritual and natural, it is the empowerment of what one can expect from life in God. It is when the principles of Scripture are sown into the hearts of family members and friends that allow them to experience covenant relationship with God. Too many people in the inner city, even in the Church, see themselves in terms of their pasts, their upbringing, their shattered marriages, their lost jobs, and their lack of adequate finances. Establishing a new covenant that will span many generations is what I am calling people within the inner city to embrace and seek after.

I am calling the inner city to reconciliation and restoration. They have chosen to live life on the dark side of this world, now the clarion call is for them to cross over the threshold of despair and unbelief into the realm of possibilities and under the power of God's new covenant. The Word of God has committed to us the ministry and the word of reconciliation (2 Cor. 5:18-19). The Greek word for reconciliation in these verses is *katallage*, meaning exchange or restoration to favor with God. Part of this occurs as we are transformed by the renewing (renovation) of our minds (Rom. 12:2). Webster's Dictionary says that "renew" means to restore, rebuild, reestablish, renovate. This renovation is found in covenant relationship with God through His son Jesus.

When I teach the establishment of generational covenants at my ministry, I am directing the thrust of my teaching toward the parents. Children learn by example and the parents must begin to exhibit the outward manifestation of the inward work of Christ. In essence, they must begin to see themselves in the light of their purpose. Clark H. Pinnock in his book, *Three Keys to Spiritual Renewal*, says that, "Jesus preached the coming of the Kingdom of God which included a vision of what life (you) under God would be like." He continues by saying, "Jesus invited people to participate in the new order which was dawning in Him and called together a new community which would live according to the Kingdom. Both by His life and His teachings, Jesus deepened our understanding of what God in His law requires. He placed great emphasis upon responding to those in any kind of need and devoted a great deal of His attention to shaping a new kind of human being."[7]

A new kind of human being operating under a new covenant. This is what I describe to every individual in my congregation (especially parents) as the springboard to reversing strongholds of the past and reversing parental mistakes. I have come to know many parents who have become Christians after they have raised their children without godly counsel and understanding. Some become Christians halfway through the parenting process and make the grave mistake of trying to shift gears from reverse into overdrive without letting the Holy Spirit work the clutch. Over zealousness under your new covenant is as harmful as having no covenant at all. As you can see, the pendulum can swing to both extremes. I understand their enthusiasm and I applaud their strong convictions to not see their kids in generational bondage, but it is critical to be lead by the Holy Spirit and informed by the Word of God in the proper approach to correcting this very sensitive situation.

There isn't a time I've had a counseling session with a parent who hasn't been heartbroken to see sons and daughters paying the price of their own mistakes. What grandparent has not been grieved to see their children repeating their mistakes while raising their own little ones? Is this not the sins of the parents being visited upon their children generation after generation? Here's the reality that they all must face before they can begin establishing a new covenant that will seed into many generations to come, they cannot go back and erase these mistakes any more than you can erase the mistakes made by the adults in your childhood. But just as they can dissolve the negative effects from mistakes made in their early life through the power of God's Word, they can do the same thing with the effects of the mistakes impacting their children and grandchildren's lives today.

The Scriptures teach that Christ gave us the authority to "bind" and to "loose." So as the parents begin to cover their children in prayer and in the Word, they also can make covenant over their children with God by binding their children to the will and purposes of God for their lives. Bind them to the truth and the blood and the mind of Christ. Bind their hearts to a desire to know Christ and the things of God. Bind their feet to paths of righteousness and bind them to the full work of the cross in their lives. Now that's covenant praying. That kind of binding places that child under a covenant umbrella that will be hard to shake by any generational stronghold. There is another part to this covenant prayer, "loosing." As the Holy Spirit begins to work with you, begin to loose specific attitudes in your children as He reveals them: wrong attitudes toward money, towards God, towards other family members. As the Holy Spirit reveals, loose specific patterns of wrong thinking and attendant strongholds such as unforgiveness, bitterness, materialism, anger, suspicion, ect. Loose wrong desires and motivations from them. Again, this is achieved through covenant praying. In addition to covenant praying, the parents must be an example of God's will in the earth.

As I conclude this chapter, God's order for parents should be duly noted. Generational covenants are sealed, I believe, in the most succinct, yet comprehensive summary of a parent's calling. This calling is found in a single sentence, which the Apostle Paul wrote to the church in Ephesus: "Do not provoke your children to anger, but bring them up in the discipline and instruction of the Lord" (Eph. 6:4). The Apostle thus summarizes God's Order for parents under the aspect of three basic commands: *Love*, *Discipline*, and *Teach*. It is under the auspices of these three basic commands that generational covenants are established. It is also these three basic commands that are missing from within our inner cities. Hence, we find their negative counterparts: *Hate*, *Chaos*, and *Ignorance*. As the young people would say today, it's time to flip the script on Satan, and enforce the new covenant that is privileged to all generations through the work of Christ on Calvary's cross.

Endnotes

[1] Bonner, Mickey, *Spiritual Warfare Manual*, (Houston, TX: self, 1983), p. 42.

[2] Bonner 42-43.

[3] Hickey, Marilyn, *Origin of Generational Curses*, (Charisma Magazine, 1993), p. 12.

[4] Haggard, Ted and Hayford, Jack, *Loving Your City Into The Kingdom*, (Ventura, CA: Regal Books, 1997), p. 105.

[5] Wagner, C. Peter, *Wrestling with Dark Angels*, (Ventura, CA: Regal Books, 1990), p. 77.

[6] Perkins, John M., *Beyond Charity*, (Grand Rapids, MI: Baker Books, 1993), p. 22.

[7] Pinnock, Clark H., *Three Keys to Spiritual Renewal*, (Minneapolis, MN: Bethany, 1985), p. 58-59.

CHAPTER FIVE

Empowering The Seed

The Impact of Proper Leadership and Positive Role Models

When you understand the social ramifications that contributed to the substandard conditions of the inner city then you will understand what must be done in addition to fervent prayer, changed lives by the power of God's Word, and the renewed awareness of the dearth that exist in the modern day "byways." The Scriptures strongly admonishes us to understand that *"What good is it, my brothers, if a man claims to have faith but has no deeds? Can such faith save him? Suppose a brother or sister is without clothes and daily food. If one of you says to him, 'Go, I wish you well; keep warm and well fed,' but does nothing about his physical needs, what good is it? In the same way, faith by itself, if it is not accompanied by action, is dead"* (James 2:14-17, NIV). In essence, there is a call for us to move beyond the initial stages of Christianity. We must move beyond prognostic and rhetorical Christianity and begin to provide *works* of leadership empowerment and role model imaging.

Jim Wallis's classic book *Agenda for Biblical People*

suggests that Christ's life-style of caring for the needy was in fact calling for a "new order" that is "at odds with the values of the world."[1] He continues:

> *The apostle James well described the difference between living faith and empty faith. Dead faith bears no fruit, shows no evidence of transformation. The criterion to judge faith is the quality of the believer's life as a living witness (demonstration) to the Gospel, not mere assent to doctrine and creed. In the Gospel of Luke, Jesus rebukes those who call Him Lord but fail to demonstrate obedience: "Why do you call me 'Lord, Lord' and do not what I tell you?"*[2]

I'm a firm believer that *works* set authentic Christians apart from imposters. The inability of the Body of Christ to unify what we believe and what we act out has immensely damaged our credibility as Christians and has opened the door to all sorts of religions, sects, hip hoppers, and filmmakers to vie for the hearts and souls of our urban youth. We need authentic Godly leadership within our inner cities and role models who are truly concerned about the future impact they have on the next generational seed. As I expressed in the beginning of this chapter, the inner cities have not always been in this condition. In order to better understand what is needed in reference to leadership and role modeling, it would be best served if we took a quantum leap back in history to identify what happened.

Taking a brief look back at the exodus from the inner city, we see the cause and effect of social and economic ruin. Simply put, all it took was the extraction of the capable neighbors, those who would have provided proper guidance and ideal role models. The process of creating substandard school systems would be to withdraw the students of achieving parents. To create a culture of chronically dependent people, merely extract the upward mobile role models from the community. Add to that the many reasons for this new breed of poverty: government dependency, the legacy of racism, the moral and spiritual decay of which drugs, crime, and violence are a symptom; and of course, disintegration of the family. All of these have contributed immensely to our urban (inner city) problems.

John Perkins said something that strikes right at the heart of the dilemma, "Many of our best trained minds—our moral, spiritual, and social leaders, the professionals, college and school teachers, and other upwardly mobile people previously forced to live in all-black neighborhoods, where maids and business owners alike lived on the same street—could now move up and out in search of a better life. These leaders had been the stabilizing glue that held our communities together. The exodus of their families, their skills, and their daily civic and moral leadership hastened the unraveling of the inner city, leaving a vacuum of leadership."[3] We desperately need this vacuum filled in the "byways." It is difficult to find individuals who live in suburbia that will come into the inner city to provide leadership and role modeling. Even if there were, I believe the most impactful leaders would be those raised from among them. I believe that is why God has called me to the inner city. God spoke to me to name this ministry *G.E.M. (Generational Empowerment Ministries)* because my mandate was to discover the diamonds in the rough and chip away at the rough edges to expose the persons of purpose they were to become. In essence, to see the individuals occupying the "byways" as God saw them, and then to point them to the divine mirror so that they can see for themselves their true identity.

This requires that you believe in indigenous leadership development and that you are willing to pay the price to see it come to pass. One of the reasons that developing leaders among the inner city dweller is so difficult is because of the price to be paid. No one wants to pay the price and the price, simply stated is, long-term commitment. To believe in their ability to lead themselves is to believe in the inherent dignity of the people who need developing. Contrary to popular belief, leaders are not all college graduates and born with a certain socio-economical status. I concur with Pastor Myles Monroe who says that, "Leaders are ordinary people who accepts or are placed under extraordinary circumstances that bring forth their latent potential, producing a character that inspires the confidence and trust of others."[4] The dearth of the inner city groans for such persons to come forth.

The impact of such leadership would serve as a beacon of light in the lives of individuals who have written themselves out of the pages life as being significant and having a purpose. As I've heard Dr. Monroe say on many occasions, "The greatest tragedy in life is not death, but life without a reason. It is dangerous to be alive and not know why you were given life." The true leader would illuminate the pathway of the "byways." He or she would satisfy the deepest craving of the human spirit and that is, to find a sense of significance and relevance. Believe it or not, the need for significance is the major cause of the destructive fruit found in the inner cities. Many suicides and attempted suicides owe their manifestation to this compelling need. Ex-drug dealers and abusers, ex-prostitutes, ex-gang members, have all confessed to me in counseling sessions that their antisocial behavior was contributed to a deep innate desire to feel important or to experience a sense of self-worth.

They felt this way because they had no one to guide them to God's truth about themselves. They were, as the Apostle Paul would say, ignorant. Listen carefully as Paul admonishes the brethren in Rome, "Now I would not have you ignorant, brethren, that often times I purposed to come unto you that I might have some fruit among you also, even as among other Gentiles." Paul wanted them to *know* that they were as important (significant) as others to whom he ministered. Without the *knowledge* that Paul was as concerned about them and wanted to produce valuable fruit for the Kingdom in Rome, they may have felt excluded from what God was doing in the earth at that time. I sense that same mind-set in the modern day "byways."

Leaders are sent to destroy such ignorance and to show them the truth. Ignorance is our most powerful enemy in the "byways." It causes wars, poverty, fear and worry. It also destroys families. According to Webster, ignorance is the "the quality or condition of little knowledge, education or experience; unawareness." When we use ignorance to describe our understanding of purpose, it means that we have little knowledge, education or experience concerning the reason for our existence. We are blindsided to the motive for God's creating us and to the end toward which our existence leads. We are unaware of His plans and purposes for our lives, and our existence becomes a trial and error game. Such ignorance is dangerous because it permits the possibility that we will live all our lives and never know why we lived.[5]

It has been said that, "Where purpose is unknown, abuse is inevitable." This is clearly seen in the inner cities around the nation. Purpose is the father of motivation and the mother of commitment. When societies, communities, friendships, marriages, and churches lose their sense of purpose and significance, then confusion, frustration, discouragement, and disillusionment, whether gradual or instant, reign. The individuals caught in the matrix of such a dilemma are out of touch with the values, morals and convictions that build strong families, secure communities, healthy societies and prosperous cities. Leadership's purpose and impact therefore, is to dissolve the ignorance, to halt the abuse, to stop the death and demise of purpose and personal fulfillment, and to speak life into the desolate places of the cities where unto they are called.

Speaking Life into Their Future

King Solomon gave us a very profound proverbial truth when he said, *"Death and life are in the power of the tongue"* (Prov 18:21). This proverb instructs us as to the importance and power of words. As leaders we are to speak the power of life into their future and death to the failures of their past. We are to speak the promises of God to the masses and let them find hope in His Word. One of those promises is in Isaiah 42:16, "And I will lead the blind by a way they do not know, in paths they do not know I will guide them. I will make darkness into light before them and rugged places into plains. These are the things I will do, and I will not leave them undone." The following lines from an unknown author capture the power of this promise:

> Child of My love, fear not the unknown morrow.
> Dread not the new demand life makes of thee;
> Thine ignorance doth hold no cause for sorrow,
> For what thou knowest not is known to Me.
>
> Thou canst not see today the hidden meaning
> Of My command, but thou the light shall gain.
> Walk on in faith, upon My promise leaning,
> And as thou goest, all shall be made plain.
> One step thou seest: Then go forward boldly;
> One step is far enough for faith to see.
> Take that, and thy next duty shall be told thee,
> For step by step thy God is leading thee.
>
> Stand not in fear, thine adversaries counting;
> Dare every peril, save to disobey.
> Thou shalt march on, each obstacle surmounting,

For I, the Strong, shall open up the way.

Therefore go gladly to the task assigned thee,
Having My promise; needing nothing more
Than just to know where'er the future find thee,
In all thy journeying—I GO BEFORE.[6]

It is with such powerful words that leaders will empower, inspire, and breathe life into the desolate soul. Life represents "hope." Eric Fellman says that, "Optimism that can become Hope is one of the foundations of spiritual potential." He further states that, "Hope is best seen rising out of despair, and despair is the everyday reality of many people who find themselves behind in the game of life, sometimes even before that game has really begun."[7] Speaking hope on a continual basis will effect the way people think about themselves and their situation. It's here that Paul places much emphasis: "Do not conform any longer to the pattern of this world, but be transformed by the renewing of your mind. Then you will be able to test and prove what God's will is, His good, pleasing and perfect will" (Rom 12:2). Edify is the word used in relation to the role of the saints as we interact with one another. The word edify means "to build up" or to "lift up."

James Allen had some thought provoking insights on this topic. He said, "A man can only rise, conquer, and achieve by lifting up his thoughts." Allen continues by saying, "Man is made or unmade by himself... by the right choice and true application of thought, man ascends to the Divine Perfection; by the abuse and wrong application of thought, he descends below the level of the beast. Between these two extremes are all the grades of character, and man is their maker and master."[8] When one absorbs the jest of what Allen is saying, with sobriety of course, one can't help but to acknowledge the power of words and thoughts. If we as leaders are speaking constant life (hope) into the lives of people and they, in turn, process it properly into their mind; powerful, life-changing effects will result.

God is looking for vessels He can use to empower and inspire lives for Kingdom work. As we look over the fields of the inner city, it is quite obvious that the harvest is plentiful but the laborers are few. My heart cry this day is that prayers will begin to flow heavenward so that the Lord of the harvest will send laborers (leaders, role models) to reclaim our inner cities and rescue the perishing.

Endnotes

[1] Wallis, Jim, *Agenda for Biblical People*, (New York, NY: Harper and Row, 1978), p. 33.

[2] Wallis 33-34.

[3] Perkins 73.

[4] Monroe, Myles, *Becoming A Leader*, (Lanham, MD: Pneuma Life, 1993), p. 7.

[5] Monroe, Myles, *In Pursuit of Purpose*, (Shippensburg, PA: Destiny Image, 1992), p. 127.

[6] Arthur, Kay, *As Silver Refined*, (Colorado Springs, CO: WaterBrook Press, 1997), p. 189.

[7] Fellman, Eric, *The Power Behind Positive Thinking*, (New York, NY: HarperCollins, 1995), p. 36.

[8] Allen, James, *As A Man Thinketh*, (New York, NY: Grosset & Dunlap, n/a), p. 5.

CHAPTER SIX

Seek The Peace

Why Should I Care?

We should care because every person needs a sense of personal identity or worth. The inner city dwellers are in desperate need of this personal identification among other things. And maybe you are thinking that you have your own problems to contend with, and wondering what you are going to get out of this deal? You get to rescue families; these are your brothers and sisters. I'm aware that the same negative mindset exists in families as well; the selfishness and inability to see beyond our own needs and rights. Larry Christenson had somewhat of an enlightening position on this matter. In his book, *The Christian Family*, he said, "Every person needs a sense of personal identity or worth. But we live in a time of great confusion and contention over the question of one's worth." He continues by saying that, "The overall emphasis in much of this is upon one's *rights*. A person has a certain number of rights that he can claim because he's worth something. God begins at a different point. He begins not with our rights, but with our duties."[1]

It is with this duty that we are called upon to care for

others. Many are turned away from ministering in the inner city because of the "risk factors" involved. In fact, I've attended many seminars on what they termed as reaching out to "at risk teens." Not only were they referring to the teens but they were also identifying the teens' communities and lifestyles. Personally, I don't embrace that identification when I am ministering to them on behalf of Kingdom, I refer to the conditions and the community as "low risk, high grace." When you make the focal point an act of service in the name of Christ, the challenge is significantly lowered: With this focal point the average follower of Christ can participate. There is a heavenly call for those who have a common divine placement in our inner cities that are dominated by a pagan mind-set. He who has an ear let him hear the prophetic call of God to pray for the "peace" (i.e., the well-being) of our cities.

As I stated in the introduction, we are instructed in Scripture to seek the peace and welfare of the city where God has sent us, "for in its welfare you will find your welfare" (Jer.29: 7, RSV). God's mandate is for us to care for our cities, especially to those we are called. If the peace and welfare of the city is one of God's concerns, then this should be at the top of our priority list of things that are important to the Kingdom of God. I'm a firm believer that the challenge of the inner city ministry is the challenge of the church to adopt cities, especially urban centers, where 80 percent of the population now lives, as its primary mission field. Inner city ministry is no longer an undertaking of a select group of liberal social activists. It now represents the most urgent item on the church's agenda, requiring specialized cross-cultural strategies and innovative approaches.

The inner city should be at the core of our passion because we should feel what God feels. We are His people... called according to His purpose. God's heart is always with the downtrodden, with people who cry out for deliverance, justice, equity, and peace. God's record of compassion is clear throughout biblical history, and so is the mandate for those who would be called children of God. For those who seem content with personal piety, the prophet Isaiah admonishes,

> *Seek justice,*
> *Encourage the oppressed.*
> *Defend the cause of the fatherless,*
> *Plead the cause of the widow.*
> (Isa. 1:17)

It is not enough to practice our religious rituals (fasting and praying inwardly). True spirituality is the expression of one's faith in action. Notice how the prophet Isaiah records God's chosen fast,

> *Is not this the kind of fasting I have chosen:*
> To loose the chains of injustice
> And untie the cords of the yoke,
> To set the oppressed free
> And break every yoke?
> Is it not to share your food with the hungry?
> And to provide the poor wanderer with shelter—
> When you see the naked, to clothe him,
> And not to turn away from your own flesh and blood?"
> (Isa. 58:6-7)

What a powerful charge to God's people! In the end, God says that they are our own flesh. In essence, would you treat your own flesh this way? Then why would you not care for others whom God has connected and identified as a part of our body? God forbid.

There is a connection between welfare and peace. I'm reminded of the words of Jesus, which were spoken as an indictment against Israel,

> *"And when he was come near, he beheld the city, and wept over it,*
>
> *Saying, If thou hadst known, even thou, at least in this thy day, **the things which belong unto thy peace**! But now they are hid from thine eyes.*
>
> *For the days shall come upon thee, that thine enemies shall cast a trench about thee, and compass thee round, and keep thee in on every side,*
>
> *And shall lay thee even with the ground, and thy children within thee; and they shall not leave in thee one stone upon another; because thou knewest not the time of thy visitation."*
>
> (Luke 19:41-44)

Embrace the connection, "the things which belong unto thy peace." I believe that "the things" represent the welfare of the city (provisions, protection, and purpose). What I see here are the essentials of what the field of psychology call, "the human predicament." Man's basic needs are the need for significance and security. I believe that these are things that belong to your peace. When these basic needs are met, peace becomes a by-product. In the Kingdom of God, peace is the assurance that you will not be forsaken in any area of life; it is dependent on your faith.

We should have faith in the fact that God wants to establish peace in our inner cities. He anticipates our needs and always stands ready to deliver us. But His desire is for the church to be the agent of change, the agent through which He has purposed to participate in the affairs of mankind. Evangelical churches, more than mainline churches, have traditionally been out to, what we have come to term as, "save souls" and "sanctify hearts." Biblically, what the church should be about is the reconciliation of the whole person to the God of peace who sanctifies wholly (I Thess. 5:22). God is supremely concerned about the healing of the body, the cleansing of the soul, and the perfecting of the spirit in order to save the whole person from sin and dysfunction. The Old Testament simply uses one word to embody this truth: *shalom*.

Shalom is sometimes translated "peace," "prosperity," or "welfare." The concept points to the abundant life of joy, fullness, health, blessing, and friendship with God. *Shalom* means to be physically well, emotionally sound, and spiritually whole. The purpose of ministry in the city is to bring peace and wholeness to people's lives. Jeremiah prophesied to the exiles in Babylon, "Seek the peace and prosperity of the city to which I have carried you into exile. Pray to the Lord for it, because if it prospers, you too will prosper" (Jer. 29:7). "Seek the *shalom* of the city" is the word of the Lord for urban Christians today. For in its *shalom*, you will find your *shalom*!

George Webber wrote, in his book, *Today's Church: A Community of Exiles and Pilgrims*, "In seeking the welfare of the city, pilgrims pray that they might be signs of shalom, hints of God's kingdom, the first fruits of God's promises." One way to view the role of the church is as a community of exiles and pilgrims, en route to the city of God. As we journey in faith, our ministry is to witness to the *shalom* that is available here and now. Webber continues, "Where there is hunger—seeking to feed, where there is sickness—seeking to heal, where there is loneliness—offering our love without any ulterior motives."[2] This, my friend, is the heart of Christendom to me. According to the words of Paul to the church at Galatia, it is our responsibility:

"And let us not be weary in well doing:
For in due season we shall reap, if we faint not.

As we have therefore opportunity, let us do good unto all men, especially unto them who are of the household of faith"

(Gal 6:9-10)

In order for the us to do this, we must leave our old methods of brochure evangelism behind, emerge from our secure places of worship and penetrate the inner cities to initiate our mission of rescue and preservation. When you use the word "seeking," as we have in this chapter, it implies movement within darkness or blindness, in pursuit of that which is not (at the present). Rescue requires seeking, and seeking requires light. Once rescued, the state of freedom must be preserved. Preservation, according to Scripture, requires a dual-purpose agent referred to as salt. Its dual purpose is to season and preserve. Jesus requires us to be both in this world, light and salt. In the same, *sermon on the mount,* where Jesus used the light as a metaphor, He also said, "You are the salt of the earth," describing His disciples.

Light makes visible that which cannot be seen. One could very well say that light is vision, and vision is defined as the redemptive revelation of God for His people. To seek the peace of the inner city, we need to first seek God for His redemptive revelation of the city. Once we have the "rescue mission" and its plans in our hearts, we will need the potency of the Holy Spirit and the preserving power of the Word of God to seal what will be delivered into our hands. When looking at our life in ministry, in regard to the two metaphors mentioned in Jesus' *sermon on the mount,* it is easy to differentiate between the two. But I'd like to draw your attention to His description of us as, *the salt of the earth.* I think this will put into perspective the depth of our role in this world (particularly the inner city). In the ancient world salt was a vital staple, both as a preservative and as a seasoning. The first function was particularly critical, since it was the only preservative available. Farmers would slaughter animals, carve the meat, and then rub raw mineral salt into it until the flesh was penetrated and the salt was dissolved. This prevented the meat from decaying.

When it came to seasoning with salt, the principle of penetration also applied. If it was to flavor the food, salt had to penetrate and be absorbed. Just as meat exposed to the natural elements of air and sun will decay, so society exposed to the elements of the evil in this world will decay. For this reason, Christians (you and I) are to be "rubbed" into culture, penetrating every aspect of life and preserving and seasoning the society in which we live.[3] When we sprinkle salt, it leaves the container. When God sprinkles His salt (people) they must leave the steeples and stained glass windows (container). We must be rubbed into the highways, and the byways (inner cities). Gone are the days when Christians would wait for the lost to adorn their doorsteps looking for the God they serve. It is now time that we "go ye into the world and preach the gospel to the poor." That was the disciples' mandate from Christ then, and this is our mandate from Christ now.

C. Peter Wagner magnifies the mandate of Christ to mankind and how we are to participate in the overall plans of God. He says that, "Some things God does by Himself; some things He does by using human beings. It seems, for example, that the difference between fertile and barren soil is basically a matter of divine providence. The ripening of certain harvest fields at certain times can be attributed only to the sovereignty of God. 'I planted, Apollos watered,' writes Paul, 'but *God gave the increase*' (1 Cor. 3:6, italics added)."

Wagner continues by saying, "God brings the harvest to ripeness but He does not harvest it. He uses believers to accomplish that task, and He is glorified when His people 'bear much fruit' (John 15:8). He is particularly interested 'that your fruit should remain' (John 15:16). But how does this fruit come? The servant of God can bear fruit only if the branch abides in the vine. Jesus is the vine, and we are the branches."[4] The harvest of the inner city is ripened, the burden of seeking the peace, the redemptive revelation, and the preservation lies on our shoulders of divine participation. Seeking the peace that God desires for our cities' wastelands, resides in our becoming salt and light in the earth. It requires us to stay connected to the vine.

As I close this chapter, it must be made clear that although I have not used the term evangelism, that is exactly what this chapter embraces, in fact, that is what this entire manuscript is about, the heart of evangelism. There is another topic that goes hand and hand with evangelism that we shall take a look at in the next chapter and that topic is *intercession*. I know it may seem as though I've put the cart before the horse, metaphorically speaking, by addressing the aforementioned topics before dealing with *intercession*. I intentionally chose this path because diagnosis always precedes treatment and preparation before surgery. Anyone involved in any form of evangelism must bathe themselves in intercessory prayer.

The process of intercession must be preceded by diagnosis or as Reinhard Bonnke states, "Intercessory prayer needs a target—God's target. That means we must know God's concern, for He knows what is happening when we do not, and is well aware of where Satan is mustering his attack."[5] Not only do we need to know where Satan is mustering his attack, we need to know what weapons (strongholds) is he using. As you can see, seeking the peace of your city is quite an involved affair. The welfare of those in the inner city requires the collective Body of Christ to seek its peace according to the redemptive revelation that God has predetermined for it.

Endnotes

[1] Christenson, Larry, *The Christian Family*, (Minneapolis, MN: Bethany, 1970), p. 204.

[2] Webber, George, *Today's Church: A Community of Exiles and Pilgrims*, (Nashville, TN: Abingdon Press, 1979), pp. 93, 94.

[3] Colson 359, 360.

[4] Wagner, C. Peter, *On The Crest Of The Wave*, (Ventura, CA: Regal Books, 1983), pp. 120, 121.

[5] Bonnke, Reinhard, *Evangelism By Fire: Igniting Your Passion for the Lost*, (Dallas, TX: Word, 1990), p. 215.

CHAPTER SEVEN

Prayer: Entering The Secret Place For The Work Of Ministry

"He that dwelleth in the secret place of the most High shall abide under the shadow of the Almighty.

I will say of the LORD, He is my refuge and my fortress: my God; in him will I trust."

(Ps 91:1-2)

I saved the topic of prayer for the last chapter because of its importance. As the old saying goes, "The best is saved for last." There is a great revival coming to the inner cities around the nation, a "great awakening" of sorts. Having studied church history, the one consistent aspect of revivals or awakenings of the past was prayer. Prayer births revival. Once continuous and fervent prayer is forgotten, the impetus of the revival is lost and all that is left is the momentum of the past. The inner city is in great need of the birthing of revival fires, but most importantly, it is in need of men and women who are bathed in and broken by prayer. Those who maintain constant poise in the secret place of the most High. Those entering into urban ministry must realize that this work of ministry is a deeply spiritual endeavor. It involves personal prayer and revival, which will lead to compassionate intercession for others. Without being grounded in a living relationship with Christ, and our presence will be short-lived, our vision shortsighted, our motivation impure. It is my opinion that before one can engage in intercession for others, one must enter the secret place for himself for a time of introspection.

Introspection Prayer: Self-inspection, The Clean Heart Principle

Introspection is a time when you pray the prayer of David, "Create in me a clean heart, O God" (Psalm 51:10). It is a time when you open yourself up to sense the urging of the Lord to surrender your total self for the work He's called you to perform. During this time of introspection, you must allow God to touch areas of your life that will potentially hinder your effectiveness in inner city warfare. Rees Howells says it best, "Before He (the Savior) can lead a chosen vessel into such a life of intercession, He first has to deal to the bottom with all that is natural."[1] He continues by speaking of the Holy Spirit in his life and explaines his own struggle in this area. God had asked him to give all of himself in exchange for all of the Holy Spirit.

"It was not sin He was dealing with; it was self—that thing which came from the Fall. He put His finger on each part of my self-life, and I had to decide in cold blood (because) He could never take a thing away until I gave my consent. Then the moment I gave it, some purging took place."[2]

This is where the sincere individuals who have a burden

for the inner city need to be spiritually. This is a place of brokenness. I have been in ministry for over twenty-one years and I have come to know that God cannot use a person who is not broken and completely surrendered to Him. A lack of brokenness causes a person who is used by God to become proud and arrogant. However, when a man is broken, his heart resists pride. Therefore, he can be used to a greater degree. Nothing is more destructive than a vessel of God who operates in the work of ministry in a spirit of pride. Success (especially in inner city ministry) is based on the grace of God. We cannot do anything on our own merit, but by His divine grace we can do all things.

Prayer and introspection breed humility in the inner city minister. The intensity of the inner city requires that we must be willing to follow the Lord in costly discipleship. The forces of darkness have gathered to oppose the gospel and the work of God. Like Goliath of old they are defying the armies of the people of God (1 Sam. 17:10). Will a David arise in our generation to say in effect: "Who is this uncircumcised Philistine that he should defy the armies of the living God? The Lord who delivered me from the paw of the lion and from the paw of the bear, will deliver me from the hand of this Philistine" (1 Sam. 17:26, 37). Ungodliness and injustice stalk our inner cities. Let us call for and spearhead a return to brokenness, humility, and submission under the mighty hand of God. Let us not permit false ideological politics of the left blind us to our God-given mission. "Righteousness exalts a nation"—therefore, let us move in the direction of Christian reconstruction, beginning with brokenness (the demolition of self) that can only be obtained in the "secret place" of prayer.

In the past we all have witnessed fallen ministers and folding ministries simply because they avoided the lesson of brokenness. People only want to know how to be successful. Yet, I have learned that success does not come by learning easy formulas or principles of ministry: we must learn the secret of brokenness, in the secret place of prayer, which gives us more grace. It is that grace that grants us ultimate success. Job was a man who learned this lesson. "I was at ease, but he hath broken me asunder" (Job 16:12). In understanding brokenness before God we must understand that the purpose of God is to break us not crush us. God's desire is to be the architect of a spiritual building that could properly contain His glory, a glory that is to be poured into the lives of the downtrodden.

The spiritual building that God builds in the "secret place," shall not fall, it will stand. Because it *will* stand, we are placed in a position to *take* a stand. When we do, I believe that God will bless the inner city. But taking a stand will not be easy. As soon as Nehemiah set out to restore Jerusalem, he faced opposition from those who hated the reformation he had in mind. They attacked him physically and morally; they taunted and slandered him; they lied and ridiculed him (Neh. 2:10, 18; 4:1; 6:2,6). We cannot expect any civility from the drug dealers, liquor retailers, and gun peddlers when we go after the heartbeat of their livelihood. We should not expect a host of praise from local traditional churches when we allow the downtrodden to attend service "just as they are." We should not be surprised when the chorus of ridicule comes in response to our plans to construct a generation of Kingdom warriors who don't resemble the status quo.

But opposition did not deter Nehemiah from obeying the will of God, and it did not prevent him from winning the battle. God frustrated the plans of the enemies, and the walls of Jerusalem were rebuilt in spite of them (Neh. 4:15; 6:15). And so it shall be with us in the inner cities, the modern day "byways." "Secret place" introspection cultivates stalwart conviction and spiritual steadiness. I have a vision in my heart of a great and renewed Biblical Christian movement in the inner city, purifying the wastelands of community, revitalizing in it, life and zeal for social change. Can we be optimistic about the inner city's future? Can we hope for a renaissance of the spiritual life in the urban centers of our major cities? Yes, I think we can. The key is moving closer to the inner sanctum of the "secret place." At this point, we have dealt with the issues discovered in introspection and our heart has been purified, cleansed for the work we must do in the inner sanctum of the "secret place" of intercessory prayer.

Intercessory Prayer:
Waging War In The Heavenlies For Your City

The enemy has a strategy for every ministry, a strategy for warfare. We are in a holy war for the souls of men and women. We are wrestling in heavenly places against an enemy who is ruthless in his desire to steal, kill and destroy. He is a master strategist who wants to pervert God's design. He has undermined the rule of the Kingdom of light and established his thrones and dominions. And one of his greatest weapons is passivity on the part of believers. While we have been busy in the churches he has been carefully instituting his rule in the inner cities of this nation, yes, even the world. As the body of believers rise to the occasion and face the fact that it is we who are responsible for reaching the lost souls in the world, we will put on the spiritual armour of God and take our place in battle.

Intercessory prayer is a militant prayer. S.D. Gordon spoke of this military prayer language:

> "The greatest agency put into man's hands is prayer. And to define prayer one must use the language of war. Peace language is not equal to the situation. The earth is in a state of war and is being hotly besieged. Thus one must use war talk to grasp the fact with which prayer is concerned."

He continues by saying,

> "*Prayer from God's side is communication between Himself and His allies in enemy country. True prayer moves in a circle. It begins with the heart of God and sweeps down into the human heart, so intersecting the circle of earth, which is the battlefield of prayer, and then goes back again to its starting point, having accomplished its purpose on the downward swing.*"[3]

This spiritual battle is described in 2 Corinthians 10:3-4, "For though we walk in the flesh, we do not war according to the flesh. For the weapons of our warfare are not carnal but mighty in God for pulling down strongholds." The intercessor must understand and identify their source of *might*, once this is achieved, we can possess the land over our cities. E.M. Bounds says that, "Natural ability and educational advantages do not figure as factors in this matter; but capacity for faith, the ability to pray, the power of thorough consecration, the ability of self-littleness, an absolute yearning and seeking after all the fullness of God—men who can set the Church ablaze for God; not in a nosy, showy way, but with an intense and quiet heat that melts and moves everything for God."[4]

When we possess the land over our cities, we gain control of their political, physical and spiritual arenas. This is because rulership of these areas is really based in the heavenlies and not in earthly places. As we pierce the darkness over our cities, more and more of God's light and glory will pour into them. Ephesians 3:10 says, "…To the intent that now the manifold wisdom of God might be made known by the church to the principalities and powers in the heavenly places…" We, the Church, are to make known God's manifold wisdom to the principalities and powers ruling over our inner cities. Intercessory prayer places us in that realm of *knowing* the manifold wisdom of God and gives us the authority and the power to take our cities back, restoring our original mandate to "subdue" and have "dominion."

The inner cities, the modern day "byways," are groaning for the sons of God to come forth with power and reclaim them for the Kingdom. We must enter into the secret place of the Almighty and pray for and over the territories to which we are called. Stake our claim and walk by faith expecting to conquer and possess the land. In his book, *Prayer: Key To Revival*, Dr. David Yonggi Cho (pastor of the largest church in the world, Yoido Full Gospel Church in Seoul, Korea) shares an amazing story of intercession. He recalls, "In 1964, I met a lady who shared with me her experience of interceding for our church. After founding my first church outside Seoul, I pioneered a church in the downtown area of our nation's capital. Twenty years before I started the church in Seoul, the lady saw three visions of the church. After each vision, she would intercede for us in the Holy Spirit. When she was praying in 1944, we were still under Japanese occupation and there was no thought of our church. Yet, the Holy Spirit knew that this church, called the Sudaemoon Church because of the area in which it was located, would become the Full Gospel Central Church."

He further explains that, "God used this faithful woman of intercessional prayer to cause the Holy Spirit to brood over that area, years before the vision came to pass. Just as the seed brings forth life in the human plane of existence, so also the Holy Spirit carries within Him all of the dynamics of life when He broods over an area."[5] I was literally moved upon reading of this woman of prayer, faith, and humility. Nations, cities, and regions are opened up to the gospel because of this kind of breakthrough intercession. Without the warfare of intercession, these areas will remain closed to the truth. People will continue to suffer and fall prey to the sifting effects of the principalities of Satan.

By The Way

As I close this chapter, I can't help but rehearse the vision God gave me for the inner city of the Palm Beaches. When I first entered the city and made known my intentions to other leaders (hoping for an integrated ministry effort), some believed their city already had enough churches, and said that they only needed to revive existing ones rather than build new ones. That, in and of itself, sounds stimulating and even admirable, but the grim reality is that many of the present churches will not receive new things, often fighting against a fresh move of the Holy Spirit. As a result, many of the present churches are ineffective. This is why I do not focus on the number of churches in an area, but on the number of churches that are having an *impact*. Often the number ranges from few to almost none.

The inner city needs visionary churches that choose not to play it safe but to take risks and trust God in starting new and innovative ministries. Because of the changing needs in our cities around the nation, new ministry approaches is imminent. Anyone sensitive to the things of God can feel the wind of the Spirit of God is blowing in a new direction. William Shakespeare once wrote, "There is a tide in the affairs of men." In these words, he was expressing his observation of the turning pages of history and their influence upon our lives. Current events dictate that our generation is caught in a swirling tide of providential events. Change is upon us, and the wind of the Spirit is blowing. During such times, many concern themselves with petty issues of tradition in an attempt to weather the storm of change. But I concur with the words of Carl F. George, in his book, "The Coming Church Revolution", he says; *"What counts is where the wind of the Spirit is blowing and whether I catch that in my sail."*[6] Prayer will keep us on course and the wind of the Spirit in our sail.

Endnotes

[1] Grubb, Norman, *Rees Howells, Intercessor*, (Fort Washington, PA: Christian Literature Crusade, 1983), p. 88.

[2] Grubb, p. 40

[3] Gordon, S.D., *Quiet Talks on Prayer*, (Pyramid Publications, 1967), p. 27.

[4] Bounds, E.M., *Power Through Prayer*, (Grand Rapids, MI: Baker Book, 1972), p. 127.

[5] Cho, Paul Y., *Prayer: Key To Revival*, (Dallas, TX: Word Publishing, 1984), p. 80.

[6] George, Carl F., *The Coming Church Revolution*, (Grand Rapids, MI: Baker Book House, 1994), p. 15.

CONCLUSION

What Meaneth This?

The Problem, The Mandate, and The Paradigm Shift

What does it mean when particular segments of our society are overlooked? Forced to face the fact that people, human souls, are just blatantly forgotten. The inner city is such a place. I call it the modern day "byways." It is apparent that not only have our government and society turned their backs on them, churches are guilty of neglect as well. I asked the question, why have local congregations not adequately responded to the challenge of the inner city? After all it was the Church that was commissioned by the Lord to care for lost souls. I believe it is because the Church has lost its missionary zeal. She has become a cold and Pharisaical organization rather than a thriving, life-giving organism. But there is a shift in the spirit realm that suggests a new engagement in ministry has been ushered in with the 21st century.

By The Way

Cheap Talk and No Labor

All words and no deeds characterize the mentality of the modern Church. Those who are attempting to minister in 20th century paradigms are fossilizing as we speak. They represent the segregated church, believing that certain cultures belong with their own socio-economic classes. This belief pretends to care about the emotional and social comfort of the inner city people, but in reality, they are distancing themselves from what they would call "undesirables." Sure they talk a good game and may even contribute to some charitable cause as a way of clearing their conscience. But to embrace the souls of the inner city as brothers and sisters would challenge lofty heights of piety, and their actions, to say the least, would echo the familiar saying, "There's no more room at the inn."

I believe that God is guiding a new fold, with new shepherds and building His Kingdom with those who have answered the call to the by-ways. He will raise them up in this day to show forth His glory and to let the world know that there are those who still care! The fragmented social structure will begin to meld together and form the mirror image of what Christ originally intended. The "byway" sheep will become a light that cannot be hidden and those who rejected the call to the poor will stand back in wonderment and know that it was the Lord's doing and it is marvelous.

Restoring Dashed Dreams

I've witnessed the mentality of the inner city; there you'll find discouraged dreamers. Individuals who once had the world at their fingertips now have their backs against the wall of life. They see no way out and their children are inheriting their despair. I see very few churches making real impact in the city where I am called. The suburban min-

Conclusion

istries are not extending their hand out to give them a hand up to a better life. In fact, because they don't live among them, they feel as if everything is "ok." Jeremiah had some indicting words for the priests and prophets of his time: "They dress the wound of my people as though it were not serious. 'Peace, peace,' they say, when there is no peace." As you can see, even in Jeremiah's time they were saying things were "ok" when the opposite was true.

The Church is called to more than just introducing these precious souls to Jesus. We are also called to restoring their dreams, encouraging their pursuit of purpose, and breathing life into their barren souls. It is time for the "sons of God" to come forth and show them the way to what belongs to them, to show them their future. This is an enormous task, but recognizing the end results should thrill us. The greatest task of dusting off dreams along the "byways" are getting individuals to understand that their perception of themselves is in direct contrast with God's perception of them. When they realize this, you immediately sense the change in their disposition. Their level of confidence rises several notches and suddenly they get a glimpse of the hope that once evaded them.

Healing Inner Conflict

After salvation, there are many issues confronting those in the inner city that must be dealt with in the arena of counseling. For the pastor in the inner city, counseling is a way of life; it is a large part of his responsibilities. This could be a major reason / variable of why the inner city is avoided by many aspiring pastors. Pastors who minister in the inner city will need to rethink their approach to resolving the personal struggles of these lost souls. They will need to consider training in counseling to be more effective in their quest to nurture lives and to bring balance to their emotional and spiritual well-being. I consider this to be a part of the "renewing your mind" process.

Preserving The Seed

The preservation of the next generation is dependent upon the rescue and renewal of the present generation. I have often said that my objective in ministry is to win my generation and influence the next. If we don't, we will find ourselves in the same dilemma as Israel, "…And there arose another generation after them, which knew not the Lord, nor yet the works which he had done for Israel" (Judges 2:10b). The reflection of today's inner city is a very close depiction of Jeremiah's summation of Israel's spiritual condition. But all is not lost; God has reserved a remnant for their deliverance. It is time for the breaking of generational strongholds and the establishment of generational covenants. This is a call for the parents of the children to raise the standard in their own lives and lead their children by example. We must enlighten the parents of the next generation of inner city youth to the importance of personal and spiritual empowerment. They must realize the power of parental affirmation and the power of words. They must know that it is their responsibility to cover their children in prayer and impart God's Word into their lives.

Empowering The Seed

I have said to my congregation that leading by example is the loudest message anyone can preach. There is such a leadership dearth in the inner city. The only role models the youth of the inner city can personally connect with are drug dealers and users, prostitutes, and absentee fathers. This is where the body of Christ must step up to the plate and be an extended family to these young people. Show them the flip side of making choices, the proper way. Show them the way

Conclusion

of reason according to the counsel of God. We must move beyond prognostic and rhetorical Christianity and begin to provide *works* of leadership empowerment and role model imaging. The exodus from the inner city by upward mobile families and churches, that could have been a positive influence, left this void in the inner city and the results have been devastatingly felt since that time.

Seek The Peace

Seeking the peace in our inner cities is to our best interest. Jeremiah states it this way, "...seek the peace and welfare of the city where God has sent us, for in its welfare you will find your welfare" (Jer. 29:7 *RSV*). When we seek the peace and welfare of our cities we will discover that the root of the problem is feelings of insignificance, lack of future hope, and no sense of personal well-being & security. We finally realize that the problems of the inner city are not plural but singular. We find that the real problem is *ignorance*. They exist in the ignorance of identity as to who they really are and ignorance to their hope, which is found in Jesus Christ.

As we found that there is one problem, we have also found that there is one cure. Jesus Himself said that Israel forfeited the things that belong to their peace simply because they did not discern Him as their awaited Messiah (Matt. 19:41-44). Seeking the peace for our inner city requires us to assist in the discernment of Christ as Messiah to those who are lost. For in finding Him, they will find themselves and abandon the "old man" and his nature and take on the image and assurance of Christ.

Prayer: Entering The Secret Place For The Work Of Ministry

Before entering the trenches of the inner city, it is imperative to understand that, other than the Word of God, prayer is your only defense against the principalities and strongholds you will face. The secret place is a place of preparation, first, for personal introspection and secondly, for outreach warfare. You must enter this battle with a clean heart, if you don't the enemy will know it and use it against you. The repercussions of ministers entering warfare with tainted hearts have been staggering over the past decade. Men and women who were once powerhouses for the kingdom have fallen and lost their ministries. Satan is crafty and knows exactly what will break you. The "secret place" is where you allow God to reveal those "hard to see" and "hard to deal with" places in our life that Satan has targeted. When we emerge from the "secret place" bathed in humility and righteousness, we are then equipped to do warfare on behalf of others in the inner sanctum of the "secret place."

There is war in the heavenlies and the battle plans are changing. The wind of the Spirit is blowing to the strategic mind of God. Are we ready to let our sails catch the flow and move with the currents of God's purpose in the earth? The "byways" are depending on our submission to the move of God. Those who have an ear to hear what the Spirit is saying to the Church and those who have a heart of flesh yield it to the hands of God that you may feel the compassion He feels for the modern day "byways."

APPENDIX

Poetry Inspired "By The Way"

Over the years a distinctive of my experiences in the inner city (the byway) has been the ability to express the dearth found there in poetic expression. The following pages are original poetic pieces birthed from my observations and personal interaction with those to whom I minister. I have chosen only a select few from my poetic manuscript to add breadth to this project. They are the voices of souls crying in the wilderness of despair.

By The Way

That Which Is Mine

I die daily a thousand deaths,
Only to triumph life's
Illusory web.

These deaths within
Resurrect a new life,
The one tradition conceals,
The one almost found at the
Edge of an ending dream.

Arising, I see ahead of me…
I see forming that which is
Now possible…
Happiness…
A breath without pain…
My due.

Appendix

Cumi Ethios Anthropos
(Arise Black Man)

Awake oh black men of my time!
Open your eyes from dreaming King's dream.
With frustration do you search, longing
Fulfillment, inner freedom, honor, and respect...
Till you dare to dream your dreams,
Pursue your purpose,
And find your place
In this world.

Arise oh black men of my time!
Put on your strength and stand.
Your women, your children... they await the
Prophesy of your time, knowing the fabric of
Their future harmoniously intertwine
With yours.

Take eagle's wings oh black men of my time!
In flight you'll soar...
Soar above the stormy delusions of hopelessness
To see the dawn of a new day... your day.

Oh black men of my time!
Stand not idle as crime, drugs, and revolt
Destroy your children in your presence
As overthrown by strangers,
Lest the life sacrifice of our
Patriarchs be in vain...

Cumi (arise).

By The Way

Forbidden Fruit

Eye pleasing
Mind beguiling;
Stimulating emotions
Inhibited and reserved.

A mirage of uniqueness
Extraordinarily alluring,
Offering untapped pleasures
And power saying,
"Come, let us delight ourselves."

Curiosity resurrected;
Inner conflict present,
Self-desire confronts soul-resistance…
A battle of wills.

With seducing lips,
Hearts turn aside;
Wills yield
Hastening…
As a bird to the snare,
Not knowing the cost.

Appendix

Lost Generation

Inheriting varying standards and
Values in its blood, their soul
Is in a state of unrest.

Lacking equilibrium and a
Center of moral balance...
No room to grow,
No inner strength to be found.
Having no concept of interdependence,
No counsel or resolve in making
Decisions... they doubt the freedom
Of their "Will."

Disorder and experimentation
Characterizes their commandment for living
And skepticism has become their
Spiritual expression.

Like a storm cloud overcharged with the
Question marks of life, they ask...
> *"Is there not plenty of time?*
> *Does not time have time*
> *For my wandering "Will?"*

Drifting aimlessly through life,
They no longer value their
Moment in history. Surrendering
Body and soul, bright futures become
Misdirected in darkness... abusing their
Purpose and earth's substance. Confused and
Angry, they stand amidst the wilderness of life
Awaiting hope's scarce voice.

By The Way

Relativity

Though it seems
I walk alone
With no purpose or
Contribution,
I am here, I am felt,
I count and
I am somebody.

Staring into a mirror
Feeling lost, misplaced;
Like a dusty forgotten
Ancient artifact buried
Beneath the earth's
Crust,
I am here, I am hidden,
And I am one of value.

Judge me,
Ignore my existence
This you may, yet;
There's no way
I'll be forgotten,
Like time, space and
Beauty,
I am here and I am relative.

Like a smooth pebble tossed,
I will skip across the
Waves of life, stay
Afloat, ignore the
Sharks and paddle on,
On to other shores

Appendix

Because…
I am here,
I am felt,
And am
Somebody.

By The Way

Clouds Speak Silently
(A metaphor of life)

They amass themselves
At various altitudes
Like fluffed snow white
Cotton balls,
Absorbing the moisture
From sky's face.

Basking in victory's
Solitude, with silent
Reverence... they speak.

Reminding us that
Peace is possible,
Claiming its most
Perfected state after
The storm, the calm;

Remitting a soft, sweet
Smell of promise, a
Promise that it will
Again rain.

Bibliography

Allen, James. *As A Man Thinketh*. New York, NY: Grosset & Dunlap.

Anderson, Leith. *A Church For The 21st Century*. Minneapolis, MN: Bethany House, 1992.

Anderson, Neil T. and Quarles, Mike & Julia. *Freedom From Addiction*. Ventura, CA: Regal, 1996.

Angelou, Maya. *I Shall Not Be Moved*. New York: Random House, 1990.

Arthur, Kay. *As Silver Refined*. Colorado Springs, CO: WaterBrook Press, 1997.

Barclay, William. *The Letter to the Corinthians*. Philadelphia: Westminster, 1975.

Bonner, Mickey. *Spiritual Warfare Manual*. Houston, TX: self, 1983.

Bonnke, Reinhard. *Evangelism By Fire: Igniting Your Passion for the Lost*. Dallas, TX: Word, 1990.

Bounds, E.M. *Power Through Prayer*. Grand Rapids, MI: Baker Book, 1972.

Bruno, Thomas A. *Take Your Dreams and Run*. South Plainfield: Bridge, 1984.

Cho, Paul Y. *Prayer: Key To Revival*. Dallas, TX: Word Publishing, 1984.

Christensen, Michael J. *City Streets City People*. Nashville, TN: Abingdon Press, 1988.

Christenson, Larry. *The Christian Family*. Minneapolis, MN: Bethany, 1970.

Colson, Charles. *The Body: Being Light In The Darkness*. Dallas, TX: Word Publishing, 1992.

Commencement speech at Harvard University, 1982.

Dawson, Christopher. *Christianity and the New Age*. Manchester, N.H.: Sophia Institute, 1985.

Fellman, Eric. *The Power Behind Positive Thinking*. New York, NY: HarperCollins, 1995.

George, Carl F. *The Coming Church Revolution*. Grand Rapids, MI: Baker Book House, 1994.

Gordon, S.D. *Quiet Talks on Prayer*. Pyramid Publications, 1967.

Grubb, Norman. *Rees Howells, Intercessor*. Fort Washington, PA: Christian Literature Crusade, 1983.

Bibliography

Haggard, Ted and Hayford, Jack. *Loving Your City Into The Kingdom*. Ventura, CA: Regal Books, 1997.

Hickey, Marilyn. *Origin of Generational Curses*. Charisma Magazine, 1993.

Hilliard, I.V. *Mental Toughness for Success*. Houston: Light, 1996.

Jeeves, Malcolm A. *Human Nature at the Millennium*. Grand Rapids, MI: Baker, 1997.

Leitch, Donovan. *Little Church*. Famous Music Corporation, 1973.

McMinn, Mark R. *Psychology, Theology, and Spirituality In Christian Counseling*. Wheaton, IL: Tyndale, 1996.

Minirth, Frank B. & Meier, Paul D. *Counseling and The Nature of Man*. Grand Rapids, MI: Baker, 1982.

Monroe, Myles. *Becoming A Leader*. Lanham, MD: Pneuma Life, 1993.

Monroe, Myles. *In Pursuit of Purpose*. Shippensburg, PA: Destiny Image, 1992.

Nee, Watchman. *The Normal Christian Church Life*. Anaheim, CA: Living Stream Ministry, 1980.

Perkins, John M. *Beyond Charity*. Grand Rapids, MI: Baker Books, 1993.

Pinnock, Clark H. *Three Keys to Spiritual Renewal*. Minneapolis, MN: Bethany, 1985.

Wagner, C. Peter. *On The Crest Of The Wave*. Ventura, CA: Regal Books, 1983.

Wagner, C. Peter. *Wrestling with Dark Angels*. Ventura, CA: Regal Books, 1990.

Wallis, Jim. *Agenda for Biblical People*. New York, NY: Harper and Row, 1978.

Webber, George. *Today's Church: A Community of Exiles and Pilgrims*. Nashville, TN: Abingdon Press, 1979.

Williams, Preston. "Urban Evangelism: A Call for Compassion." *Church of God Evangel*. 1991.